JAYSON

*J*AYSON

The true story of a 20 year old Blue Jay

Vicki Formato

Published by
CEM Ventures, Ltd.
Harwich, Massachusetts, U.S.A.

To purchase additional copies of this book, please contact CEM Ventures, Ltd., at the above address, or call (508) 896-4988, toll free (866) 246-7800, fax (508) 896-2586, email: cemventures@yahoo.com

On the web: www.JaysonTheBlueJay.com

FIRST HARDCOVER EDITION
First Printing, September, 2004

Designed by Vicki Formato

Printed on acid-free paper.

ISBN 0-9760072-0-7

Jayson's story is dedicated to my husband and to my five children. They have been understanding and supportive of the bird and me for all these years.

Jayson's story also is dedicated to my six grandchildren – Christopher, Emily, Mia, Victoria, Alexa, and Haley. I love seeing the joy on their faces as they prepare the little blue jay's "gourmet breakfast" and are then held up to the cage to watch the bird eat.

I would be remiss if I did not thank the many selfless people at the Wildlife Clinic and at the Rehabilitation Center who have helped Jayson survive all these years. They are truly to be admired – this book also is dedicated to them.

CONTENTS

Prologue

Unexpected things happen in everyone's life. Some are good. Some are bad. Some help you learn and grow, and others just make life harder. But whatever happens, I do believe there is a reason.

Jayson is a small blue jay. This little bird hopped into my life twenty years ago – at a time when my five kids and two dogs made life complicated enough that the last thing I wanted, or needed, was another animal. Why me? I lived in a nice residential neighborhood with many houses, and Jayson could have gone to any one of them. Yet the small, frightened bird chose mine. I often wonder what would have happened if Jayson had gone somewhere else instead.

In looking back, Jayson has been a very good thing in my life, and I am thankful to have had the bird for all these years. My efforts to help this helpless creature have become a twenty-year long learning and growing experience. Jayson, the small blue jay, has made an indelible mark on me, on my family, and on the lives of many other people.

Jayson, 20 July 2004

1

The Neon Sign

*"Blue Jays are among the most intelligent and
opportunistic of North American birds..."*
— *North American Birdfeeder Handbook*

I have often thought to myself that
there's a neon sign over my house, one that only
animals can see. I can only imagine what it says –
"Free Food," "Warm Place to Sleep," "Strays
Welcome," "Stay as Long as You Like,"… The
notion of the "neon sign" goes back many, many
years to when my husband, Richard, and I were first
married. Animals would either show up at our
house, or my husband would bring them home.

This is the story of one of those animals,
without a doubt the most unusual one – *Jayson* –
the two-ounce blue jay that hopped into our lives in
August of 1984, and has been with us ever since.

The time has come to tell Jayson's tale – I do hope you find it interesting.

Piewacket

But before telling you about Jayson, a bit of history is in order, looking back some thirty-seven years to the summer of 1967. Our first visitor was a mangy, wild, white longhair cat that my husband picked up one night driving down a heavily wooded road. He spotted the cat darting between bushes by the side of the road, obviously distressed. Needless to say, Richard managed somehow to get the cat, and we, the newlyweds married only two weeks, had a new pet in a no-pets apartment. Actually, it was an attic apartment in a private home, and the landlord lived downstairs, which led to some interesting problems. We kept the cat in the bathroom, put in a litter box, and placed an ad in the newspaper to find her a good home. Even though she was only a temporary visitor, Richard named the cat Piewacket, after the cat in the movie *Bell, Book and Candle*.

Of course, Piewacket had no idea of what a litter box was – she was, after all, wild – and chose instead to do her business in the bathtub. After coming upon this unpleasant surprise, my husband, always the engineer, devised a "solution" – he would make a plywood cover for the bathtub, thus discouraging Piewacket from using it as her toilet. Of course, this required buying plywood, and tools, and drawing detailed "plans," blueprints would be my guess. My idea, instead, was to fill the tub with a couple of inches of water. That worked very nicely...

Finally, after two weeks of interviewing prospective new families – yes, Richard actually did this – Piewacket got a good home. My husband even checked a few weeks later to make sure the cat was happy. The Piewacket episode is typical of how my husband interacted with animals, and was a precursor of how these animals would affect our lives. I was becoming conditioned to expect the unexpected when it came to animals, and I always wondered what would come home next, and what turmoil the new visitor would bring.

Over the next nine years there was a steady stream of strays that Richard somehow managed to find (a dump kitten, a gas station dog, a dog found wandering the median on the turnpike...), all of which were placed in good homes or returned to their owners. By 1976 we had four kids and a dog, and our lives seemed to be on an even keel, that is, until the day I walked by a pet store. Bringing home animals wasn't always my husband's doing...

"Beast" and Mr. Spock

I desperately needed a clothes dryer, and one day set out to buy one. While I was shopping, I walked past a pet store that had on display the cutest German shorthair puppy (I grew up with shorthairs...). In spite of my better instincts, I went in, just to look at the dog. But by the time I left the store, I had made up my mind – she was mine! I wanted her. If necessary, I was even willing to forgo my dryer. Now all I had to do was convince Richard. I knew he probably wouldn't be too keen on the idea, because, among other things, the puppy did not need "rescuing." Perhaps the biggest issue, though, was our dog, a Beagle named Mr. Spock. His ears were quite the opposite of the Star Trek character's, hence his name. Would the puppy and Mr. Spock get along? How would Richard and the kids feel about another dog?

When I broached the subject of the shorthair, my husband's reaction, very much to my surprise, was "Okay, you can get the dog, but not at the price the store wants. Talk them down." What I didn't realize at the time, was that Richard figured I

4

never would haggle over the puppy's price. It's not my nature. He knew that. This way, he would acquiesce, and I would forget about the dog. But that isn't what happened. I went back to the store, struck up a conversation with the owner, and negotiated a "very good" price for this adorable, three month old pooch. When I told Richard about my success, he laughed, told me how surprised he was, and agreed that now we had a new dog. And, yes, I got the dryer, too...

I went back to the pet store to fetch my new puppy, and as I was writing a check for the "very good" price, the store owner told me he was glad to see her go. As it turns out, my cute little pooch nearly had destroyed his store. One night she somehow escaped from her cage and left the place a shambles. She knocked over many of the items in the store, including a couple of fish tanks, and gorged herself on dog bones. The store owner's view of the dog was much different than mine, and I must admit I thought twice about going through with the purchase. Of course, in the end, I did. And I'm glad that I did.

My new puppy immediately won my heart, especially when she squeezed herself between me and the car seat, quivering all the way home. I knew then that she "needed" me, and I felt good about taking her away from the store. Her given name was Annabelle, but that soon morphed into "Annabeast," and eventually just "Beast." That's what the kids called her.

Annabelle ("Beast")

While my kids loved our new puppy, Mr. Spock merely tolerated her. She was frisky, and he was much older and growing tired. Besides, Annabelle seemed to be on a mission to torment him. One of her best tricks was crouching behind a door and pouncing on him as he walked by, which irritated Spock to no end. But, as Beast lost her "puppyness," she and Spock became friendlier, and would frequently share a rug in front of the wood stove.

Beast and Jayson

It was 1976 when I purchased Beast, and she was with us eight years later when Jayson arrived in 1984. Jayson and Beast had a very precarious co-existence, because, after all, German shorthairs are bird dogs, and Jayson is a blue jay. The natural tension between them was evident right from the beginning, and it persisted until Beast passed away in 1990. In 1992, we got another German shorthair whose name was Abigail. In a rather curious twist, Jayson and Abigail eventually came to work together in an unusual partnership, even though I never would have expected it. Watching them play off one another turned out to be quite fascinating...

1984, a Banner Year

We always had at least one dog, sometimes two, in addition to the requisite fish tank. In 1977 we finally were able to buy a house of our own in a very nice residential neighborhood. There were lots of kids in the neighborhood, but, interestingly, not that many animals, at least not many pets. Our family grew to five kids, and between them, our dogs, and the fish, and all the neighborhood children who hung out at our house, it was a very, very busy place. During the early 1980's we settled into a routine, if hectic, lifestyle that had little room for any more family members, especially non-humans.

For most people living in the suburbs, we had more than enough pets. We had lost Mr. Spock – he died in 1979 – but he was followed by more fish, several newts and, some time later, by Butch the lizard. And, of course, Beast was still with us. But, no, not in our case would this be enough. The "neon sign" was still there, shining as brightly as ever, and in 1984 two special animals saw the sign, came to the house, stayed with us, and made permanent marks on our lives, and on the lives of many other people.

Baron Sees the Neon Sign

Late in 1983, Baron, a German shepherd, showed up, hanging around the back yard, and playing with the kids. Unlike most of our furry visitors, Baron wore a collar, with tags no less – maybe our luck was changing. Baron wasn't a stray, and we didn't want another dog. We called his owner, a girl named Jeannie who lived in town in a rented house a few miles away with several other young women. Jeannie became a friend, because Baron became a regular visitor. But, as if

Baron

predestined, a few months later, the house Jeannie rented was sold. And she and her roommates were unable to find a place that would take a big dog. She asked if we would adopt Baron, which, needless to say, we did. So in May, 1984, we were back to two dogs, Beast and Baron. Baron became one of our dearest pets, yet he was not the best example of the neon sign at work...

Jayson sees the Neon Sign

This story is not about Beast, or Baron, or any of our other animals. It's about Jayson, the small blue jay that came into our lives a few months after Baron, in August of 1984. Jayson definitely saw the neon sign, took full advantage of it, and by far has had the greatest impact on our lives.

I remember that day twenty years ago as if it were yesterday. It was a very hot, humid summer's day, mid afternoon. I was in the garage refinishing a piece of furniture, and my oldest son was fixing his bike in the driveway. My son ran into the garage, blurting out, "Mom, a bird just hopped by me on the driveway." We both looked out, but the bird wasn't outside – it was inside. A small, obviously confused blue jay was standing on the garage floor, sopping wet – a thunder storm had just rumbled through – squawking, sort of.

The jay hopped to within about six feet of where we were, and simply stood there, occasionally squawking. It wasn't the raucous "jay-jay" squawk we all have heard. The squawk was similar, but not as screechy, and, as the little bird squawked, it would extend its wings slightly and they would quiver. As soon as the squawk ended the wings were tucked back in. The little bird wasn't trying to fly – the wing movements were part of the squawk. Over time I would come to understand that this was Jayson's "help me" squawk, which is quite different from the bird's alarm squawk.

The bird's behavior was extremely odd. Wild birds don't hop into garages, and they certainly don't get close to people. I suspected the bird might be injured. So I picked up a wicker basket and placed it over the bird. It actually let me get close enough to do this without flying off, which only heightened my suspicion that something was wrong. Because it was a Sunday, I decided to feed the bird, check it carefully in the morning when the light was better, and either release it or, if necessary, bring it to the nearby veterinary medical school to be checked out.

The next day my husband and I examined the blue jay as best we could, closely looking at it in the wicker basket. Something about the bird just wasn't right, but neither my husband nor I could pinpoint it. We did see that the bird's beak didn't quite close at the tip. But, never having seen any birds close up, we had no idea whether or not this was unusual. Of course, the bird's behavior, hopping into the garage and allowing me to get close, well, that was very unusual.

I was concerned enough that we decided to bring the blue jay to the veterinary school to have it looked at. I called to ask where I should bring the bird, and was told to go to the "wildlife clinic," a special unit that dealt only with injured wildlife. The clinic's existence was the first example of serendipity in Jayson's life, and, believe me, there are many more. So, off to the wildlife clinic the blue jay went...

The Wildlife Clinic

The folks at the clinic were very accommodating, and totally committed to taking care of injured wildlife. After being "admitted," the jay was brought to an exam room. To this day, Jayson has a "chart" at the wildlife clinic. Richard and I waited, taking in the variety of wild animals that were patients at the clinic. One veterinary student walked by with a seagull completely wrapped in a towel, with only its foot sticking out (yes, we asked...). Another was feeding baby opossums with an eyedropper.

On the way into the clinic, there were large rehabilitation aviaries for injured birds of prey – mostly eagles, hawks, and owls – marked by signs warning visitors away. I would find out later that the reason for the signs was to prevent the birds from "imprinting" on people. The aviaries' residents were being rehabilitated for release back into the wild, and too much interaction with humans could jeopardize their release. A wild bird's survival depends on its being constantly vigilant. Interacting too much with humans and imprinting on people would place these majestic birds at risk. Of course, I had no way of knowing at the time that some weeks later similar concerns would apply to Jayson, the little blue jay. The wildlife clinic was a fascinating place, and a good one for what would eventually become "our" blue jay.

After a while, we were summoned to the exam room. When my husband and I walked in, the first thing we noticed was an x-ray on a viewing panel. It looked very much like a fossil imprint, and we chuckled looking at it. We soon learned, to our surprise, that it was the blue jay's. The next thing we noticed was the bird itself, sitting *very* quietly in a small stainless steel container with a perforated lid. It had been anesthetized for the x-ray and was still groggy.

The vet pointed to the x-ray and told us that, in his opinion, the bird likely was a couple of months old, probably hatched in late spring. He suspected it had fallen from its nest and was raised by a human. On the x-ray, he showed us broken bones that had healed, but not set properly. He also showed us bones that were not properly formed. The doctor explained that the bird's bone deformities almost certainly were caused by the wrong diet. Blue jay parents know what to feed their chicks – both the female and male feed them – but untrained people don't. This explanation also would account for the beak's not closing. The bird was diagnosed as having rickets caused by a dietary deficiency, primarily a lack of vitamin D.

We asked what would happen to the bird. Would it recover on its own? If not, could the condition be treated? Neither my husband nor I had any experience with birds – in fact, we knew very little about them, certainly nothing about birds that had been fed the wrong diet. The vet told us that because the bird was young, the damage might be reversible with proper diet and vitamins over an extended time. But, because of its age, the bird would require very frequent feedings throughout the entire day.

Unfortunately, the clinic could not allocate its resources to treat such a common species, especially a bird requiring such a high level of care. There was no shortage of blue jays, but there was a real shortage of resources. The clinic tended to work on more exotic animals, or on problems that

Jayson sitting on a felt covered perch in the chicken wire cage. Photo taken a few weeks after the bird saw the neon sign. September 1984.

could be addressed more directly, for example, by surgery. The little blue jay would have to go to a wildlife "rehabilitation" facility, that is, if one could be found. If none was available, the bird would be euthanized. Hearing this, we told the doctor we wanted to help the little bird if we could. Richard and I talked to him at length about our experiences with other animals to see whether or not we could do anything useful.

The vet was quite hesitant at first, asking lots of questions. As a general rule, wildlife would not be released to the care of untrained people. Richard and I had to make the case that we could work with the little bird, and we did that by describing our experiences with other animals. In the end, the doctor agreed that we could try to rehabilitate the bird so that it could be returned to the wild. Strict conditions would be imposed, and the doctor also insisted that we stay in touch with the clinic during the rehabilitation period. I probably don't have to say it, but, in keeping with the neon sign that Jayson had seen, Richard and I ended up taking the bird home, hopefully to treat its medical problems and agreeing to do everything exactly as we were instructed.

The blue jay needed a very special diet for about six weeks, after which it had to be examined again before being released. With proper nutrition there was a chance the bone deformities could be reversed. It depended on how far along the bird's bones were in their development. Because vitamin D is critical for proper bone formation, the doctor gave the bird a vitamin D injection before allowing us to take it. The rest of the bird's treatment would be through diet. We then were given very specific feeding and care instructions. It would be a lot of work, caring for this small bird, but, because of the fixed period – six weeks – Richard and I were willing to give it a try. After all, this little blue jay really did need "rescuing"…

- - - - - - - - - -

2

So, How Many Turkeys are you Starting?

*"Lots of people love 'em. Other people hate 'em.
But most people agree that blue jays are
bright, beautiful birds."*

— Ranger Rick Magazine

Few people have the privilege
of observing a live blue jay up close. They are
strikingly beautiful birds, with brilliant, deep colors.
Most birds are predominantly one color, but not so
the blue jay. Blue jays sport many colors, from
gorgeous shades of blue, to bright white, to black
and gray. As we drove home from the wildlife
clinic, I had the luxury of studying the jay as it sat
quietly in the back seat in its wicker basket. The
basket was loosely woven, and the bird readily

visible. It was a very bright day, a bit chilly because a cold front had moved through the previous afternoon. The crisp air and brilliant sunlight really brought out the little bird's spectacular color. I was captivated simply looking at it.

But my study soon was interrupted by my husband's asking where we would keep the bird. He was rambling on about how the wicker basket wasn't big enough. I remember something about "too deep and not enough surface area." Richard quickly came up with a plan – he would build a cage. And, while one part of me thought that this might not be such a good idea, the other part agreed with him that buying a large cage for a six-week visitor wasn't justified. While Richard kept mumbling about cage designs and dimensions, I was more focused on the bird's diet, especially the fact that I would be responsible for feedings and routine care.

The vet had explained that only an aggressive diet therapy held out any chance of reversing the bone deformities. This meant not only feeding the bird frequently, but also giving it only the proper food. Of course, if I were the mother or father blue jay, my chick's balanced diet would consist of fruits, berries, seeds, bugs, worms, small invertebrates, and all sorts of other foods, because blue jays are omnivores, and that's what they typically eat. Over time, Richard and I would learn just how omnivorous blue jays really are.

Because nature's diet was not available, the best blue jay food at this point, according to the doctor, actually was dog food. The vet recommended several brands of high quality canned dog food, each containing a good balance of the nutrients the little bird needed. As it happened, we already used one of the recommended brands for our own dogs. But dog food alone was not enough. The little jay also required vitamins and minerals. The wildlife clinic supplied us with a powdered supplement to be mixed in with the dog food. And there was yet another ingredient, "turkey starter." We were given a recipe with precise proportions for mixing, and were told that any feed store would have turkey starter, a nutrient-rich food formulated specifically for young poultry.

The First House

That afternoon my husband constructed a large cage. We wanted something big enough for the bird to fly around without feeling too confined, yet be safe from the dogs. The cage was about three feet long by two feet high and two feet deep, made from a heavy gauge wire mesh, the kind used for garden fencing to keep out critters. Richard bought a roll at a local garden supply store. When the cage was done, one of the first things I noticed was the size of the mesh openings, roughly two inches high by an inch wide. They seemed large, maybe too large. My concern was that the bird could squeeze through and get out of the cage. Richard's answer was "Look at the size of the bird compared to the size of the holes. The bird can't fit." At the time neither of us appreciated just how much of a bird is nothing but feathers.

I was in charge of interior decorating. The cage needed some sort of solid floor for the blue jay to walk on. The doctor pointed out that the bird's feet were slightly deformed. The jay could perch, and in fact did, on a twig placed in the wicker basket for that purpose. But I was worried that the bird might have trouble walking on a hard surface because of the foot problem. So I lined the cage with a piece of foam rubber left over from one of the kids' school projects (serendipity at work again...). I also had Richard fabricate a shelf in one corner of the cage, which also was covered with foam. This gave the little jay a higher place to sit, since birds prefer high places. The final additions were a couple of wooden dowel perches running from front to back, giving the bird some "tree branches" to sit on and fly between. In the end, Richard and I were very pleased with the "house" we had built for our newest guest.

Jayson's "first house," the chicken wire cage the bird lived in for about six weeks from August to October, 1984.

Finding "Turkey Starter"

While Richard was out buying cage materials he stopped at a nearby agricultural supply store, figuring he could get the turkey starter there. He looked high and low, but couldn't find it. As a last resort, he asked, and was told that the turkey starter was out back in the warehouse. The clerk asked how many bags he needed. The conversation went something like this, "One should be more than enough. How big is a bag?" The clerk's answer was "Standard size, fifty pounds." My husband laughed, saying that fifty pounds was way too much. The clerk then asked "So, how many turkeys are you starting?"

Richard replied that he was starting a two-ounce blue jay – only one – no turkeys. He needed about a cup. Could he get it there? The clerk chuckled, replying "No, we only sell turkey starter in 50 lb. bags." At this point, not wanting to buy a huge bag of turkey starter, Richard called the wildlife clinic. Naturally, they got a laugh out of his dilemma, and told him to come on over to get a cup of starter. I have no idea why we weren't given some when we were there earlier that day...

The Sunroom

Of course, with two dogs in the house, we couldn't place the cage on the floor, or even on a table. At best, the little bird would be terrified, and at worst, well, you get the idea... We expected that the dogs would be taking quite an interest in our new tenant. It was decided that the bird's temporary home would be in the sunroom that we added to the house a couple of years before. The room consisted of three outside walls with six sliding glass doors, and it was filled with plants everywhere, many hanging from the exposed ceiling rafters. It was a beautiful, sunny place, one I felt sure the little bird would like. So we hung its cage from the ceiling nestled between hanging plants. The bird now had a temporary home until it would be well enough to be released in about six weeks.

The sunroom. Jayson lived in this sunny, plant-filled space from August, 1984, to November, 1985.

Needless to say, our kids were fascinated by the new visitor, and hovered over Richard and me as the new accommodations were prepared. Our oldest was sixteen at the time, and the youngest nearly seven. News of the blue jay spread through the neighborhood like wildfire. There were at least twenty-five kids in the neighborhood, and, at one time or another, every one of them was at our house that afternoon.

A Step Up?

The kids beamed as we had a formal "moving" ceremony in which the little blue jay was carefully removed from its wicker basket, which took some doing, and gently placed in its new house. Naturally, birds don't like being picked up – and the little jay was no exception. I was a bit skittish about trying to pick up the bird, so that job fell to my husband. The little bird developed a dislike for Richard that persists to this day. Whenever Richard picks up the bird, even now, twenty years later, the jay "attacks." Sometimes the bird is pretty funny in its antics – "power pecking" my husband's fingers, and grabbing and twisting his skin. According to Richard, it is truly amazing how strong the little bird is (the bird never has pecked me...). But, in spite of this rocky start, over the years the blue jay has become more accustomed to being handled by my husband, and now tolerates it quite well.

Finally, late in the day, after much hoopla, the blue jay was in its new cage, the neighborhood kids had gone, and we were settling in for a relaxing evening with our new guest. Throughout all this, our dogs were either in the main part of the house or tied out in the yard. Neither Annabelle ("Beast") nor Baron had seen the bird... yet. When the dogs did come in, they certainly noticed the bird, especially Annabelle. But, surprisingly, they were almost dismissive of it. The dogs would look up when the bird squawked or rustled, obviously curious, but then quickly went back to what they were doing. Now, if we had had a cat, the situation would have been quite different, as it has been in recent years when my son's cat, Catzilla, visits.

The blue jay already had been fed several times, and seemed to be doing well acclimating to the new environment. While the bird got used to its new home, I turned to making dinner. I was looking forward to relaxing afterward, having been through a very long and tedious day. We always had dinner in the sunroom, which we used year-round because it had a wood stove. The table was an oversized pine trestle table, with benches for the kids and chairs at either end for mom and dad. Dinner always was eventful, but never like this one.

The "Grate" Escape

Everyone was enjoying the meal, talking only about the bird, when all of a sudden we looked up to see the blue jay squeezing through one of the holes that were "too small" to get through. Before anyone could react, the bird flew across the table just inches above our heads, and even closer to the two dogs, one of which, the shorthair, leaped off the floor with her mouth wide open. The kids screamed and yelled, while the dogs barked and dived after the bird, which had landed on the floor in a corner. My husband, who was as startled as everyone else, reacted just as instinctively. He also dived toward the bird, and, thankfully, managed to get to it just before the dogs would have.

The jay was squawking loudly, this time its alarm squawk – the little bird was absolutely terrified. It's hard to imagine that so small a bird can make as much noise as the jay did that night. I suspect that, to this day, the bird blames Richard for that frightful night. It certainly treats him as if it were his fault. Richard placed the jay back into the wicker basket, looked at me, and mumbled under his breath "Don't say a word..." Richard's dinner was ruined. He had to go back to the garden shop to get some finer mesh chicken wire, which he wrapped around the cage to form holes the blue jay couldn't squeeze through...

Jayson in the chicken wire cage.

Letting Go

The dust finally settled, and over the next six weeks we did our best to rehabilitate the bird. The jay was fed the prescribed diet eight or more times each day, hopefully to reverse its bone deformities. We also spent a great deal of time observing and interacting with the little bird. To our surprise, the jay had quite a personality, nothing like what might be expected from a wild bird. I knew we would miss the little bird when it was gone. But rehabilitating the blue jay and setting it free clearly was in the bird's best interest. Soon enough the time came to bring the bird back for its final exam before being released. The five kids were excited and sad. They had developed a bond with the bird, and thought of it as "their blue jay."

But they also understood how important it was to release the bird, so the little jay could lead the life it was meant to have. As for Richard and myself, well, we were anxious to return to a more normal life. We felt very good about doing what we could for the bird, but the fact is, caring for the small blue jay was an awful lot of work. Parting with the little bird would be bittersweet, but necessary.

- - - - - - - - - -

3

Home, Sweet Home

"Because of this omnivorousness as well as their intelligence, they have been able to survive the loss of forested land by adapting to human-made environments..."
— *North American Birds*

Setting the blue jay free was a day we wished to remember. When finally it arrived, we wanted everyone to be there to say goodbye. Richard grabbed the camera and a couple of rolls of film, planning to photograph the jay as it flew off, with the kids in the background waving and wishing it the best. Of course, with the "neon sign" controlling our destiny, none of this actually would happen.

Wild Blue Yonder?

The wildlife clinic staff had no idea we were bringing a crowd, five children in addition to the two of us. But, as usual, they were very nice about it, and allowed all five kids into the rather small exam room. The little blue jay was in its "traveling cage," which is what the bird's first chicken wire cage came to be called. The vet gently took it out to carefully study its legs and feet and its beak.

Much to my surprise, the entire exam lasted only a matter of minutes. The doctor's trained eye saw things we did not. He looked at us, shaking his head slightly, obviously disappointed with the bird's condition. The jay had just flunked its first – and only – "flight physical." The diet had worked slightly, but not well enough, the vet explained, pointing out how the bird's legs were not straight enough, its beak still not closed, and its toes still bent. He told us that from the beginning it was a long shot that the bird would recover. Everything possible had been done to rehabilitate the bird, but the therapy failed. At this point, the little jay could not be released into the wild because it likely would suffer a painful death from disease or a predator. The vet thought that at best the bird might live a few days. And besides its physical problems,

31

another risk factor was that the bird now had imprinted on humans, so it might get too close to people and their pets.

Realizing how serious the situation was, I asked the kids to step outside while my husband and I conferred with the vet. When we asked what would happen to the little jay, he told us the bird would be euthanized. Although there were rehabilitation centers for wild birds, facilities whose objective it was to return birds like the jay to the wild, in this case there was no chance of success. The bird would never be able to survive on its own. Hearing this, all I had to do was look at my husband, and instantly he knew what I wanted. Richard immediately asked the doctor if we could keep the bird – the neon sign at work again!

"Our" Blue Jay

I think the vet was quite surprised that we actually offered to care for the bird, knowing how much work is involved and the long-term commitment. He didn't respond right away, and it was clear that he had serious reservations. When finally he did say something, it was along the lines of "Well, you've done an excellent job. But do you really think you can keep it up? Wild birds require a tremendous amount of care. They're not canaries." Richard and I made our case. We were used to the bird. The kids loved the bird. The bird was imprinted on us, as the doctor had already pointed out. We had cared for the bird for six weeks, and it was doing well. Why not keep on going?

But in spite of our success so far, the vet was still unsure about our keeping the bird for what could be a very long time. Caring for a wild animal is something only trained professionals should do. I cannot emphasize enough how important it is that people not interfere with any wild animal, except possibly to bring it to a rehabilitation or veterinary care facility if it is injured.

Richard and I understood well that a wild animal never should be taken in without proper supervision, even one that is injured. There is little doubt that this is what happened to the blue jay – someone took the bird from its nest or, if it had fallen out, chose not to return it. Instead the bird was taken home and fed the wrong diet, which resulted in deformed bones. Whoever did this, however well intentioned, certainly did not do the little jay any favor. This sort of unfortunate outcome is more likely than not when untrained people take charge of wild animals. My husband

33

and I were sensitive to these issues, but we pressed on because, under these circumstances, we believed it was better for the bird.

It took a fair amount of convincing, but eventually the vet agreed that we could take the bird home on a trial basis. We could care for it as we had been doing, but only on condition that it would be returned to the wildlife clinic for periodic check-ups. If there were any problems, the clinic would not allow us to take the bird back home. It was a considerable burden, yet I felt compelled, and Richard did, too. We agreed to follow the doctor's instructions exactly, and to keep in touch. Over the years to come, the little blue jay would make many trips back to the wildlife clinic.

When all this was arranged, the kids came back into the exam room. The doctor explained to them why the bird could not be set free, and how they were acquiring a new animal friend. He told them they were fortunate to have such an unusual and beautiful bird, and also charged them with taking good care of it by following mom and dad's instructions to the letter. The kids' reaction was pure glee. They had developed a real affection for the bird and were happy to have it stay.

The vet asked if we had any questions, and the first thing the kids wanted to know was "Is it a boy or a girl?" The doctor very carefully looked at the bird, and told us that in his opinion, it was a male because of its brilliant color, which helps attract a mate. Another question was "How long do blue jays live?", and the answer was "a couple of years, for this type of bird."

After some paperwork updating the little bird's chart, we started home with our new pet blue jay. The kids' first order of business on the ride back was to pick a name. Up to now, I had discouraged naming the bird, knowing that personalizing an animal makes it harder to part with it. I fully expected that the bird would be flying off that afternoon, and, inevitably, setting it free would be hard on the kids. But now that the bird would be living with us, it did need a name. Coming up with one was a lot of fun. There was lots of discussion, most of it quite humorous, with plenty of totally outlandish names. In the end, our new little bird was named "Jayson," spelled as it is for the obvious reason.

A Bird's Home is His Castle

Now that Jayson was ours, this newest member of the family also needed new digs. The traveling cage had to go. It was ugly and unwieldy, hardly a place for a beautiful bird like Jayson. Richard again decided to build a cage, and this time not only did the plan make sense, but it resulted in a spectacular house for the bird. We looked at commercially available cages, but none was suitable. A wild bird needs a *big* cage so it can move around freely. We ended up taking the best features from what we saw and combining them with our own ideas, based on our experience with the bird, to design a cage specifically for Jayson.

The cage was three feet wide, three feet high, and two feet deep. Just above the bottom was a removable tray for easy cleaning. At the one-foot height were two front-to-back shelves that were about fifteen inches wide. Near the cage's roof, in the middle, there were two wooden perches running from front to back, and a third one in the lower left corner. As in the traveling cage, the perches would be Jayson's "tree branches."

This was the first version of Jayson's cage. In the next iteration changes were made based on how the bird spent its time. I noticed that Jayson seemed to like squeezing into corners, especially at night when he went to sleep. So, at the two-foot height, in the back, we added two small rectangular corner shelves. These provided a couple of cozy spots for the bird to squeeze into, which he did regularly. Until fairly recently Jayson always has slept either on a perch or on a corner shelf. Another change was that the lower perch eventually was removed. Jayson didn't use it much, and it interfered with cleaning.

The first wooden cage in the sunroom. Jayson is sitting on the main shelf on the right. This version of the cage included three perches, two at the top and one in the lower left corner above the clean-out tray. The corner shelf had not been installed yet. October 1984.

Jayson's doctor had warned us that the foot deformity likely would progress – eventually the bird might have trouble perching. The vet also warned us that the bird's malformed bones exposed normally protected skin on its feet to abrasion on rough surfaces. This could produce lesions that might lead to an infection. Jayson's new house was designed with these warnings in mind – all the shelves were covered with foam rubber. The foam essentially eliminated the possibility of injury from a hard or rough surface, and also minimized stress on the bird's bones as much as possible.

Because the bird had to bathe, Jayson's house included a sunken bathtub set into the foam on one of the shelves. The tub was a little over an inch deep by about six by nine inches. Its design allowed Jayson to get into the tub without climbing or perching. Because the wooden perches could harm Jayson's feet, custom-made felt sleeves were used as perch covers. They were changed every day and washed to be sure they were clean. The perch covers were blue, of course – what other color could they be? Jayson had a nifty new house, custom-designed and built for his unique requirements, and he loved it.

Getting to Know You

Over the next several months, from the fall of 1984 through the spring of 1985, we all got to know Jayson, and the bird got to know us. He also got to know his name, and responded to it, and to other key words, mostly food-related. To this day, mentioning "cookie" immediately gets

Jayson's attention, and the bird expects to get one. Everyone, especially the kids, were quite impressed. If you called the bird by name, he would chirp and come to the front of the cage, that is, if he liked you.

Jayson's first wooden cage hanging in the sunroom surrounded by potted and hanging plants.

Jayson liked some people and animals more than others, and reacted accordingly. If he liked you, you knew it. And, conversely, if he didn't, you knew that, too. Blue jays are extremely perceptive and intelligent, and these characteristics were evident in many ways. Jayson was constantly assessing his surroundings. You could tell just by watching the bird. He settled into his new environment quickly and happily, and within a short time developed a routine.

The vet told us to cover the cage around sunset, to darken it so the bird would sleep. We tried several times, but Jayson would have none of it. He would squawk if he knew we were on the other side of the cage cover (a large towel). We quickly gave up, and let the little bird go to sleep whenever he wanted to. Usually that was when we went to bed and shut the lights. Jayson would fly up to the highest shelf or perch, tuck his head under his wing, and quickly fall off.

The first time the kids saw this, my youngest one, the seven year old, was horrified – she thought the bird's head was missing. Jayson's neck is so flexible that there is no sign whatsoever of the bird's head when it is tucked in. When it came to getting up in the morning, on most days the bird was up before us, probably at sunrise. But there were some days Jayson "slept in," waking only when my husband and I rustled the newspaper over coffee. Sleeping in usually coincided with a late night the day before...

The "Tubby"

One of Jayson's favorite activities was taking a bath, his "tubby." The bird took at least one tubby every day, and frequently more than one. A careful observer could tell when the bird was about to bathe.

Jayson thinking about taking a tubby. The bird "tested" the water before jumping in and splashing around until soaked. May 1988.

Jayson would approach the tub, stick in his beak, shake it from side to side as if testing the water, and then jump in the tub with a splash. Jayson managed to get wet all over by vigorously shaking his head and wings. There wasn't a dry spot on the bird. He was quite the sight soaking wet, and I laughed every time I saw him. After a tubby Jayson's appearance simply was hilarious – he looked like he had been through the washing machine. And not only were his feathers disheveled, but he was only about a third as big. It soon became clear how the bird fit through what we thought were small openings in his first cage.

Tubby time turned out to be my oldest son's least favorite bird activity. For some reason, whenever my oldest son sat near the cage, Jayson would decide to take a tubby. The bird's splashing invariably got my son wet, who became very annoyed. This odd behavior persists to this day, even now whenever my son visits. Personally, I think it's intentional. Jayson enjoys getting my son's goat, and knows just how to do it.

Bird Physiology 101

Jayson always has spent hours preening himself, especially after a bath. He is indeed a handsome bird, and has always worked at maintaining his dapper appearance. Nature helped, too. One day, while cleaning the bird's cage – I did this every day, and my daughters frequently helped – I noticed several tail feathers hidden under the foam. This struck me as odd.

Jayson still enjoys frequent tubbies. Here the bird is sopping wet after taking one. June 2004.

While occasionally I would find a feather here or there, this time there were quite a few, enough to arouse my curiosity. I looked Jayson over very carefully, and got the impression that, besides not having as many tail feathers as usual, he actually was losing the feathers on top of his head. I made a frantic call to Jayson's doctor, believing the bird was seriously ill. The vet just chuckled, as he explained that Jayson probably was molting.

This was my first class in "Bird Physiology 101," a course in which I am still enrolled. Within a few days, my beautiful blue jay was essentially bald, and also had lost most of his tail feathers. Curiously, he didn't loose his wing feathers, or the down feathers on his chest. I suppose this is Mother Nature's way of allowing a molting bird to get around and stay warm. Jayson has molted every year since, always in the spring, and often again in the fall. I think the fall molting is unusual, probably a result of Jayson's not living in the wild.

The little bird is quite prolific at producing feathers, very beautiful ones. Because of my feelings for the bird, I never have been able to throw away even one of Jayson's feathers. To me, it would be like throwing away part of the bird. Literally, of course, it is exactly that, but they are only feathers. I suppose it's the symbolism that troubles me – so I save the feathers instead of tossing them. Through the years I have saved every one of Jayson's tail feathers, and now I have enough to completely upholster several birds.

While at first Jayson's molting was a shock, soon enough we all came to look forward to his annual or semiannual new "do." The bird looked so silly while his new feathers grew in, it was very funny, and he always looked very bright afterward, almost like a "new" bird. Jayson always has been full of surprises. Molting certainly was one of them, but not the only one. It was actually my second class in Bird Physiology 101, the class taught in the spring of 1985, that surprised me the most...

Jayson molting – the bird went "bald" first. The stubby feathers on Jayson's head are new ones growing in.

- - - - - - - - - -

4

"Girls will be Boys, and Boys will be Girls"

— Lola, recorded by the Kinks

"Monogamous. Solitary nester.
Male feeds during courtship."

— Birds of New England

"Mom, something's wrong with the bird!" These words began class #2 in Bird Physiology 101. Although I was primarily responsible for Jayson's care, my oldest daughter, then a teenager, provided a great deal of help. Birds, especially wild ones, tend to be very messy. So I did all the cleaning. My daughter, who enjoyed interacting with the bird as a pet, frequently did the feedings (some cleaning, too...). It was during a morning feeding that she noticed

46

something definitely was not right with the bird and yelled "...something's wrong..."

I immediately thought some disaster had occurred, and rushed to the cage. What I saw, instead, was Jayson sitting far back in the cage, staring blankly, very still and quiet. Having gotten to know the bird, this behavior was very strange indeed. Usually Jayson was perky in the morning, and quite hungry. Once he was up, he hardly stopped moving all day long. But now, this constantly busy little bird was almost motionless, and showed no interest at all in his food.

In the many months that Jayson had been our pet, there had been some brief episodes when he was quiet and subdued, mostly in the evening when he was tired and the lights remained on. But this time it was different. I could tell. I called the wildlife clinic, and was instructed to watch the bird closely, and if he seemed to get worse during the day, or not improve by morning, to bring him in for a check-up. Little did I know that I soon would find out why Jayson was behaving this way.

Strands of Hair

Another unusual episode occurred that day at Jayson's noontime feeding. Because he was now a young adult, Jayson's daily feedings had been reduced to three – breakfast, lunch and dinner – not counting all the snacks the kids (and we) gave him.   During the course of the morning, approaching lunchtime, Jayson seemed to improve slightly. He became a little more active, but he still wasn't quite himself. I decided to try giving the bird some lunch, to see if fresh food would perk him up.

When my daughter opened the cage to place his food tray inside, Jayson hopped on her arm, climbed up it, and started tugging at her hair. To her credit, my daughter let him do this without pulling her arm away. I was amazed at what I saw. There was Jayson, nearly at my daughter's shoulder, standing firmly, grabbing her hair and pulling it as hard as he could. The bird actually succeeded in getting a few strands. This continued for a couple of minutes, until Jayson abruptly hopped off her arm onto the foam with her hair in his beak. The bird dropped the strands of hair, went over to his food tray, and nibbled on his lunch. It appeared, thankfully, that Jayson was returning to normal and simply adding another interesting, if somewhat strange, behavior to his repertoire.

But this was not the case. Just as suddenly as Jayson had perked up, the bird reverted back to quiet mode, again becoming subdued and retreating to the back of the cage. At this point I was really worried. Not only was the bird's activity level down, but his behavior towards my daughter was bizarre. He had never before done anything like this. I decided not to wait until the next day, but instead would watch the bird for an hour or so, and bring him to the clinic if he didn't improve.

Jayson remained in quiet mode for some time. I went about my business, all the while keeping an eye on the bird. All of a sudden I noticed something in the bird's beak. I went over to the cage, and to my total shock and amazement, I saw the bird holding in *his* beak an *egg*. Jayson placed the egg on the foam toward the back of the cage. My little boy bird laid an egg! I was flabbergasted – Jayson obviously was not a *boy* after all!

Where's the Encyclopedia?

My daughter freaked out, yelling something like, "Mom! What *is* this! The bird can't lay eggs. It's a boy!" She was very upset. And I was very confused. All this time, "Jayson" was, for us, a male bird. People do personalize animals, and he was a boy, no doubt about it. He looked and acted the part, or so we thought. With his laying an egg right in front of us, there now was no doubt that "he," in fact, was "she." What had me really puzzled was how any of this could happen, that is, without a real boy bird around...

I called my husband, whose reaction was "Look it up." Richard had no idea why this was happening either, but he agreed that I had a point, a very good one. Jayson's being a female bird was something we could get used to. But laying eggs with no male bird around was a different matter. I looked in every book I could get my hands on in the house, but couldn't find an answer.

So I called the wildlife clinic. They just chuckled. The doctor's comment was something like, "Well, I was wrong. She's obviously a female. And, as I said, sexing birds is very difficult." The vet also told me that Jayson needed another food supplement containing the minerals and vitamins she needed while laying, which required a visit to the clinic to pick it up. In thinking about Jayson's new identity, it finally occurred to me that chickens lay unfertilized eggs every day. Jayson simply was doing the same thing, and that day wasn't the end of her egg laying.

While I was out getting her vitamins, I stopped at a pet store for some other supplies and was quite surprised to discover that they actually sold man-made bird's nests, I would guess as decorations. However they were used, I got one as a present for Jayson, something she actually could use if she laid any more eggs (the vet told me she probably would). But the nest didn't help. Jayson thought of it as a toy, not a house for her chicks. The bird usually would toss it off the edge of the shelf or turn it up on end. She played with it, but never used it for nesting. Over the years, Jayson had a nest in her cage for long periods of time in what turned out to be a vain attempt to help the bird feel more comfortable during egg laying. Maybe if Jayson had built the nest herself her reaction would have been different, but that never happened either.

The doctor was right about Jayson's laying more than one egg. Each day for the next three, the bird laid another egg. She bunched the eggs together in a corner of one of the large shelves, toward the back. In between eggs, Jayson reverted to quiet mode, I suppose because her body was producing the new egg. The ones that already had been laid were simply left alone, while the bird seemed to be physically and, dare I say, emotionally, consumed by the process of producing the next egg. When she was done, there were four, beautiful, tiny speckled eggs. Of course, there was no chance of getting another blue jay from these eggs because they weren't fertilized. I couldn't help but wonder what Jayson would do with them.

Scrambled Eggs, Anyone?

Jayson was one confused bird, but not for the same reason we were confused. After all, she knew that she was a female bird. She just didn't know what to do with the eggs. There was no nest. There was no male bird, no mate to help her, either with the "kids" or with the nest. I can only imagine what Jayson was thinking.

I found out the next morning, when I woke up to find two of the four eggs broken on the clean-out tray at the bottom of her cage. Whether or not she accidentally rolled them off the edge of the shelf, or intentionally dropped them, I don't know. I would like to think it was an accident, but, truth be told, I don't think so. I opened the cage to feed her, and she grabbed another egg in her beak and broke it before my eyes. I was horrified, even though I knew the egg was unfertilized. Because of this, I attempted to "rescue" the last egg, not having any idea of what I would do with it even if I managed to get it. As it happened, I failed. Jayson wouldn't allow me to get near the egg. She got to it first, and broke that one, too.

Jayson with an overturned nest in her cage. She treated the nest as a toy, instead of a house for her chicks-to-be, often throwing it over the edge of her shelf or upending it as she did here.

Nesting Nothing

Now that the eggs were gone, I figured Jayson's egg-laying episode was over. Of course, Nature doesn't work that way, and the bird again surprised me. The next morning Jayson was sitting quietly in the corner, where the eggs used to be, all fluffed up, with a placid, vacant, self-satisfied sort of look on her face. Every so often she would get up, hop over to her food tray or water dish, and take a bite or a drink. She then immediately returned to where the eggs were supposed to be, wiggle her little body, fluff up her feathers, and squat down to sit on the non-existent eggs.

Jayson all puffed up "nesting nothing."

Jayson was "nesting." But she was nesting nothing. This peculiar behavior persisted for about three weeks. I was taken by how the small bird, now a "mom," was compelled by Nature's imperative to act out a mother's role, even without the possibility of chicks. It was a truly amazing display of how strong animal instinct is. Even though her eggs were gone, she incubated the nonexistent chicks-to-be. And, when the process was complete, it just ended. She was done, and she abruptly got up and returned to her normal behavior, as if she never had laid the eggs in the first place or spent weeks nesting nothing.

What's in a Name?

During the several weeks that the bird nested the non-existent eggs, everyone continued to call her "Jayson." When Jayson finished nesting, the kids wanted to know what we were going to do. Would we give the bird another name? Should we? I think the kids wanted a name that reflected the bird's gender, which, of course, makes a lot of sense. The problem was that Jayson had learned her name well, very well – so well that by now she had a real identity. We not only called her and thought of her as Jayson, but she actually had become "Jayson." Whenever she was at the back of her cage, for example, if someone called her name, she would immediately come to the front, chirping. Jayson learned to interact with people in part by responding to her name.

In my mind, this poor bird was confused enough. Changing her name at this point would only make things worse. There was no turning back for me. Sticking her with another name was unnecessary, all the more so because of the unusual spelling we had chosen. I saw "Jayson" as a gender-neutral name, precisely because of the spelling. It could be a boy, or it could be a girl. So, after much discussion, everyone agreed that the little girl blue jay's name would remain Jayson. When anyone else asked, which happened frequently, we simply explained. The only thing I did to reflect Jayson's new status was change her perch covers – from blue to pink…

- - - - - - - - - -

5

Pining Away

*"Usually in pairs or flocks; especially
gregarious after nesting season."*
— *Birds of New England*

Blue jays are remarkably social
animals, something I learned the hard way. As the
kids got older, and bigger, we needed more room.
Our house wasn't all that large. Although it had
four bedrooms, the kids' rooms were quite small,
and we had five growing children, three of them
boys. Richard and I looked and looked for a new
house, and one day, quite by accident, came upon
one being built that had not yet been advertised.
We contacted the builder, struck a deal, and in the
summer of 1985, less than a year after becoming
Jayson's adopted "parents," began making plans to

move that fall, in November when the house would be finished.

The new house had an atrium, which we thought would be a wonderful replacement for Jayson's sunroom. In many ways, it was similar, with lots of windows and skylights, and surrounded by woods. I was sure Jayson would love the new place. The atrium also had beams for hanging plants and Jayson's large cage. The new house really seemed perfect, not to mention its having five bedrooms, big ones too.

No Ruffled Feathers

One of my main concerns about moving was keeping the bird happy. Jayson was so well settled in her new cage that she noticed even the slightest disruption of her routine or her environment. Changes often frazzled her, and she never missed a thing. As an example, whenever I put a new toy in her cage, she would become very wary. It usually would take a long time, sometimes days, for her to approach the foreign object and begin exploring it. When she was comfortable, Jayson would get close to and inspect the new object, tilting her head from side to side, carefully studying the intruder. After a while longer, she would ever so gently peck at it, I guess to see if it reacted. Maybe by pecking back? When she was convinced that the new thing posed no threat, she might begin to interact with it, usually by pecking harder. Some objects really seemed to catch her interest, while others she simply ignored. Shiny things always got her attention, but the wooden blocks my husband thought she would like – something to peck at – were a complete bust.

Jayson was also very wary of animals and people moving around her. The kids and the dogs, Beast and Baron, and, of course, Richard and I, were her "family." She largely ignored us when were going about our business, and she hers. But, if a strange person or animal showed up, inside or out, it didn't matter, the bird noticed. She reacted in different ways for reasons that only she could understand. She might become very quiet, or extremely noisy and agitated. This behavior posed a problem when it came to moving into the new house.

There was no question in my mind that having lots of people milling around moving furniture and making noise would be a major disruption for the bird. There was only one solution – we needed a moving "strategy" that minimized interfering with Jayson's normal routine and environment, at least as much as possible. So we developed a plan. My husband and I decided that we would do as much as we could away from the bird, packing, organizing, and so on. On moving day, everything would be taken out through the main house, not through the sunroom in the back. This was less convenient for us than going out the back of the house, but it was better for the bird. Jayson would stay in the sunroom until everything had been moved.

I think this plan worked well. Jayson didn't seem to become too disturbed as the house was emptied. In fact, she hardly seemed to notice. But she did become agitated when Richard placed her in the traveling cage, which we had to use because her sunroom cage didn't fit in the car. Fortunately we were moving only about five miles, so the trip was quite short. I was mildly apprehensive about the move, but all the planning paid off. The move went well, and Jayson successfully was relocated to her new home.

Where is Everybody?

Jayson had a posh location in the new house. The cage was hung high off the floor. The atrium was extremely bright, with an oversize sliding glass door, two very tall windows above it, and, on the opposite wall, two tall double windows. The slider looked to the west, and the opposite wall

Jayson's first wooden cage in the atrium in the new house. The bird is sitting on the right perch at the top of the cage. This version included a corner shelf in the upper left and still had the bottom perch. December 1985.

to the south. Jayson's room was sunny and beautiful all day long. It was full of plants, some hanging, and many in pots on the floor. The atrium was two stories, with a cathedral ceiling more than twenty feet high. It was big enough that a beanstalk-like floor plant eventually grew all the way up the wall and began curling around the ceiling requiring wall hooks for support. The kids, my husband, and I were sure that Jayson would love such a beautiful place.

Moving is hectic and stressful, in this case more so on us than on the bird. Everyone's attention understandably was focused on setting up the new house, unpacking all the boxes, settling in by putting things in their places, and trying to get what for teenagers is essential to life itself – a telephone. It seemed the only two happy people were Richard and I. The kids complained about living in "cow country," not having a phone (that took two weeks and cell phones didn't exist…), not having their friends around, and countless other "big" problems, as they saw them. My husband and I were so distracted by the hubbub, in fact, that we sort of forgot about the bird, and didn't watch her as much as at the old house. After all, she was safe and secure in the atrium, in the middle of all the plants, with a fabulous view of the woods outside. There was nothing to worry about – Jayson was happy and safe.

It was probably a week before I noticed that not all was right with the bird. Jayson had become very quiet. I didn't think she was about to lay eggs again because of the time of year. As it turns out, I would be wrong, but not right then. The bird's behavior was definitely different. Richard and I wracked our brains trying to figure out what it was about her new location that caused the problem. There was nothing obvious. So the bird again became the focus of everyone's attention. What we all soon noticed was that Jayson perked up whenever someone entered the room and got close to the cage. She more or less reverted to her usual active, noisy self. But as soon as people left, she became quiet again. There appeared to be a clear correlation, but no one noticed it sooner in the midst of the move.

Out of the Mouths of Babes

Our youngest child, who had just turned eight, asked the obvious question, "Maybe Jayson's lonesome?" Instantly I realized she was right. I had been so distracted, I just wasn't paying enough attention to the bird. When my daughter clued me in, I instinctively knew she had put her finger on the problem. Jayson really was "lonesome," in the truest sense of the word. She was pining away because she knew her family was nearby, but couldn't interact with us. The bird could hear us and see us in the adjoining kitchen, but we weren't "close" enough, which is what the bird was used to. Now the problem was, what to do?

A Labor of Love

I have no doubt that if Jayson had the run of the house, assuming the dogs didn't eat her, she would have been a happier bird. At least then her family would be nearby. Of course, both because of the dogs and for reasons of cleanliness, letting the bird loose simply was not an option. The quandary was how to get Jayson's bird cage to where the people were. There was only one solution – put it in the kitchen. But this was much easier said than done.

Our eat-in kitchen consisted of a "galley" area for cooking, and an "ell" containing the old pine trestle table. The table area also contained a sliding glass door onto the deck. It was a perfect spot for Jayson's cage. The problem was the cage's size. There was only one place it could go – a corner in the kitchen next to the slider – but it was far too big to fit. I looked at Richard, he looked at me, and together we complained about having to build yet another cage. Jayson's present house was only a little more than a year old, but already it was obsolete. Unfortunately, there was no other choice, not if the bird was going to be close to where the "action" was. I must say, my husband had become

64

quite proficient at building custom bird cages, and they were nicely done. But he wasn't exactly thrilled about having to construct another one so soon.

Of course, one advantage to building a cage from the ground up, as the *Rolling Stones* might say, is that you get what you want, or, in this case, what you need. We specifically designed Jayson's new cage to fit in the corner next to the sliding glass door. It was also near one end of the trestle table, an arrangement that gave Jayson a good view of the outdoors, and also of what was for dinner. So we built the cage and relocated the bird.

Within a day of moving into her new house, Jayson was a new bird. She was perky and busy and constantly watching and chirping. The new digs also included some new and improved features. Jayson's house was still three feet high, but now it had four shelves, three at the one foot height, and one at the two foot height. Because the cage was fit to the corner, its shape was more or less triangular, so that people could walk past without bumping. The shelves conformed to the cage's varying width, a small shelf on the right, a bigger one in the middle, and the largest on the left. Above that shelf, at the two foot height, was a small corner shelf, the kind Jayson was used to for snuggling in a corner at bedtime. Jayson now had the perfect "bird house," and she thoroughly enjoyed it.

Remodeling Done Right

The different shelf sizes worked well, because each area of the cage could serve a different purpose. The small right-side shelf contained toys and Jayson's rock. It gave her a place to play, and to do her "beak maintenance." Every day, to this day, the bird strokes her beak on the rock. I still don't know why she does this, but I would guess it is either to sharpen or to clean her beak. Jayson used the middle shelf for food and her water dish. The left-most shelf, the biggest one, contained her tubby. Jayson actually spent most of her time on the smallest shelf because that's where her toys were and where she was busiest. Another advantage the small shelf provided was a great view of the outdoors, and of the house, so Jayson always knew what was going on inside and out.

Directly across from Jayson's cage was the entrance to the family room, some twelve feet away. The television sat diagonally in a corner of the family room opposite Jayson's cage, giving her a perfect view of the TV. Jayson actually watched TV whenever it was on. She still does. The bird would be casually interested in some programs, and very interested in others. I could tell by her behavior when she was interested in certain programs. She especially liked ones with birds singing or squawking, or other animals making noises, or ones with music.

Jayson's corner cage in the kitchen eat-in area. Baron is lying on the floor in the atrium. Jayson is sitting on her upper shelf on the left next to a nest. The slider is to the right. The streamers and balloons are for a birthday party. May 1991.

Sounds play a very important role in Jayson's life, and we soon discovered many ways this became evident. One was that whenever the slider screen was open, Jayson could hear and talk to the birds outside. She developed a dialogue with them, mostly with the jays. If a jay squawked,

Jayson answered. I got a real kick out of watching the outside jay look feverishly for Jayson, but not being able to find her. The outside jay was confused. It would converse with Jayson for the longest time, sometimes as long as half an hour, hoping that Jayson would somehow materialize. Of course, she never did.

After Jayson was happily settled in and enjoying her new house, the next question Richard and I had to deal with was, what to do with Jayson's old cage? It was much too big to be used as a traveling cage, and it was too nice to simply throw away. It was also so big that very few people would want the cage in their house – after all, it was specifically designed to provide as much space as reasonably possible for a wild bird. What could we do with it?

Sometimes the obvious answer is right in front of you, but not easily seen. My husband called the wildlife clinic to ask if they had any ideas, and their immediate response was something like "Bring it over. We're always looking for bird cages. We would be happy to take it." The clinic staff was quite impressed when Richard brought in the cage. Jayson's old cage was one of the best they had and would be put to very good use. Richard and I were delighted we could contribute something to the wildlife clinic. The people there had helped so much with Jayson, we felt privileged to be able to help them in return. But this wasn't the last contribution we would be making to the clinic...

- - - - - - - - - -

6

Aliens from Mars

"They mimic the hawk's cry for no better reason, perhaps, than that they may laugh at the panic into which timid little birds are thrown at the terrifying sound."

— Birds Every Child Should Know

It is common knowledge that blue jays are raucous, shrill, loud, noisy birds. Some people dislike them because of this. But the blue jay has another side that few people have an opportunity to appreciate. Blue jays vocalize constantly, and most of their sounds are very pleasant. In this regard, Jayson is no exception. Where probably she is an exception, is that she doesn't like to perform in public.

I don't recall exactly when I first heard Jayson sing. What I do remember is that it was sometime in the fall of 1984, while the weather was still nice enough to keep the screen doors open in the sunroom. One such day I heard what I thought was a noise, but when I paid more attention, the "noise" sounded more like music. Upon listening still more carefully, I identified the sound as a bird singing. I assumed it was a bird outside, especially because I had never before heard a song quite like it. It was subdued and liltingly melodic, very pretty and quite unusual.

I knew that Jayson was listening, too, and I wondered if she would respond. I went into the sunroom to watch her reaction. To my great surprise, I discovered that it was Jayson doing the singing, not a bird outside. Until that moment, I had no idea that a blue jay could sing such a beautiful song – and it was truly beautiful. I was puzzled, and consulted the bird books for an answer. What I found there surprised me, too. The fact is, blue jays do sing beautiful songs, but most people who hear them simply do not associate them with the jay. It is a pity that the jay's reputation as a noisy, shrill bird is so deeply entrenched. I think the jay's reputation would be much improved if more people thought of it as a true "song bird."

Jayson listening to a sound she likes.

Stage Fright

That first time I heard Jayson singing and stepped into the sunroom, it took the bird a few seconds to notice my coming in. As soon as she did, she stopped singing – completely, not another peep. I have no idea why, but for some reason Jayson suffers stage fright. What is even more peculiar is that her stage fright applies only to her singing *her own* songs. If there is anyone around that Jayson can see, she will not sing her own songs, period. Any number of people can be in an adjoining room, and as long as they are out of sight Jayson will sing up a storm. But she immediately stops singing if anyone becomes visible to her. Through the years, many people have observed this odd behavior, and no one can explain it. To this day, Jayson has not gotten over her stage fright.

When it comes to making other noises, not singing her own compositions, Jayson is far from bashful. She never has hesitated to make herself known, no matter how many people are nearby, visible to her or not. Jayson's noise repertoire consists of squawking, growling, gurgling, croaking, whistling, clicking, hissing, and many other sounds too strange to describe. I can think of one difference between her making these sounds and singing her own songs that may explain the bird's stage fright.

As far as I can tell, all these other noises are made in response to some stimulus. Jayson hears something and, for whatever reason, instinctively responds to it. I think the response is so instinctive that she has no choice but to vocalize, whereas singing her own songs is a matter of choice. I may be attributing too much in the way of human characteristics to the bird, but the stimulus-response idea would explain why sounds like Jayson's noises are involuntary, whereas others, like her own songs, are not.

After observing the bird for a while, it became obvious when Jayson was intently paying attention to a sound that caught her interest.

The Highest Form of Flattery?

Besides scoring and singing its own delicate melodies, the blue jay is a fabulous mime. Jays mimic the sounds of other birds with remarkable accuracy, and Jayson is especially talented in this area. She's particularly fond of doing her duck, crow, hawk, and owl imitations. She is very good at all of them. If crows are outside cawing, Jayson invariably caws back. Just like the outside blue jays she talks to, the crows become confused, looking for another crow they can hear but cannot see. I think it's a measure of just how talented blue jays are that Jayson actually fools real crows. Of course, blue jays are part of the crow family, which in part may account for why Jayson does such a good job imitating them.

What is less clear is why Jayson makes duck sounds. We never had ducks nearby, until moving to Cape Cod, that is. I cannot imagine she ever heard a live duck before she started mimicking them. All I can think of is that she probably heard a duck on television, and liked the sounds enough to adopt them. I cannot identify exactly what sound it is that triggers Jayson's duck response, but I am convinced from watching Jayson over many years that this is a stimulus-response behavior. There is some sound that sets off her duck imitation.

75

Jayson did her crow, owl, and hawk imitations because these birds lived in the woods around the house, and she routinely heard them. They vocalized or she saw them, and she responded. In most cases her response was limited to sounding back, but not always. The best example is her "hawking," which she did much less frequently than the other bird noises, and only for a special reason. Hawking is Jayson's way of responding to seeing a hawk, usually soaring overhead. But instead of only making the hawk sound, hawking always is accompanied by crouching. The bird squats low in her cage, tucks her wings in tight, and lowers her head, all the while moving and tilting it quickly, but slightly, to keep the hawk in view.

This is a marvelous display of animal instinct, because crouching is something Jayson rarely does when making crow or other noises. Crouching is a special activity reserved for hawks or other predatory threats. Jayson instinctively knows that hawks are predators, and that she may be the prey. She tries to minimize her profile as much as possible. When the hawk leaves, Jayson quickly returns to her normal posture and behavior.

Seeing her amazing ability to "play back" such a wide variety of sounds, there is little doubt that Jayson probably can replicate almost any sound she hears. Whether or not she does is determined either by instinct or by how much she likes the sound. And Jayson's uncanny ability to accurately mimic sounds is not limited to bird and animal noises. She mimics machines, too.

Ringing with the Phone

Anyone raising kids from the early seventies on probably has watched *Sesame Street*, the children's television show on PBS. One of its funniest skits, to me at least, was the aliens ringing with the telephone. Two furry Martian puppets are looking in the window at a telephone trying to figure out what it is. The phone rings, and the aliens, obviously delighted, mimic the phone by ringing back, and bobbing as they do. I think the idea was that the aliens were happy they found another alien with whom they could communicate.

Jayson apparently felt the same way. Just as she imitates crows and other outside sounds, one day Jayson began "ringing" with our telephone. Needless to say, she did an excellent job of imitating the ringing phone. Many times Jayson continued ringing long after the phone had stopped, apparently having a grand old time while she did. What I found quite amusing is that she also "bobbed" up and down as she rang. As implausible as it may seem, I think Jayson may have learned this behavior by watching the *Sesame Street* aliens and mimicking them. The TV was in plain view for the bird, and I know she watched it. I also know she paid attention when something on television sparked her interest.

While Jayson didn't ring every time the phone did, she did ring most of the time, frequently at the most inopportune moment. Everyone enjoyed Jayson's vocalizing – it was hugely entertaining – but occasionally it created problems. In the old house, the bird's cage was in the sunroom, away from the phone. But in the new house, Jayson's cage was in the kitchen, close to the phone.

The bird's proximity to the phone created a problem because I operated a small business out of the house. Even though I had an upstairs office, there was a two-line phone in the kitchen so I could take business calls there as well. All my customers were other businesses, not individuals, and some were large corporations. My business also was a corporation, and the phone was answered with the company name. This was done very professionally. My customers had the impression that they were calling another company with the usual corporate business office. They had no idea that my small business was run out of the house, and I had no desire to let them know. This arrangement worked well for many years, until Jayson came along, that is...

The 15-Yard Dash

As you can imagine, if the business phone rang and the bird started ringing with it, I couldn't answer the phone in the kitchen. The noisy bird would be ringing in the background. Instead of taking the call, I usually would run up the stairs in an attempt to answer the phone in the office. Many times, probably most of the time, I didn't get there before the answering machine picked up. When I did manage to get there in time, I frequently was winded enough that the caller would ask if I were okay. Of course, if I happened to be downstairs and knew that I couldn't get upstairs quickly enough, I had no choice but to let the answering machine pick up. In a way, Jayson, the small bird in my kitchen, was deciding which phone calls I could take. I certainly didn't want my corporate customers to suddenly realize that they were doing business with a housewife working out of the kitchen, but that's exactly the spot Jayson put me in. What a way to run a business!

Set Up by a Bird

Sometimes Jayson was sneaky about her ringing. The business phone would ring, but occasionally the bird did not. I would wait a respectable ring or two, and if she were still quiet, I would answer the call. Every so often, as soon as I said "hello," the bird would start ringing and bobbing. I knew that most callers heard the bird – after all, she was very loud, and close to the phone. Some customers were polite enough not to ask about the noise – I could tell by their hesitation. But others couldn't contain their curiosity. Because these people were calling a place of business, I felt compelled to offer an explanation of the noise. In thinking back, my explanations all were pretty lame, silly ones like "Oh, that's my other line," or "That's the fax machine." Of course, there were some customers who would ask "Do you have to take that call?" – Jayson was that convincing...

Whenever Jayson rang with the phone, even *I* had a problem containing myself. I always was on the verge of laughing hysterically, watching the bird make phone noises, bobbing up and down as she did – it was high comedy! Most of the time I managed to control myself, but not always. I can't help but wonder, as implausible as it may be, whether or not Jayson knew what she was doing. Was this a game? If jays intentionally imitate hawks to frighten little birds, seemingly enjoying it for the sport, maybe Jayson was doing something similar with me...

"1 Ringy Dingy, 2 Ringy Dingies"
— *Ernestine*, SNL

For the longest time, my business received orders and inquiries only by mail or by phone. I sold a small plastic oil dispenser, usually in small quantities, but to a large number of customers. As a result, I received lots of small orders. As fax machines became common, customers routinely would ask if they could fax over an order. Potential customers calling for product information would frequently ask me to fax a spec sheet, or a price list, or answers to specific questions. The problem was that I didn't have a fax machine, and soon it was apparent I had no choice but to get one. Of course, there was an immediate and substantial benefit to getting one – orders or inquiries placed by fax didn't require my answering the phone. This at least reduced the problem of Jayson's ringing with the phone when a customer called.

Instead of installing another phone line, I decided to piggyback the fax onto the business phone using a "distinctive ring." The phone company provided a separate telephone number for the fax using the same line as the business phone. To distinguish regular business calls from faxes, the fax number had a double ring. The fax line rang at least a few times every day. Now I had three different rings to deal with: the regular house phone; the regular business phone, which rang with a different tone than the house phone; and now the double ring for the fax machine.

Jayson, like all blue jays, is very perceptive and precise. Naturally, being the observant and precise little bird she is, Jayson picked up on the double ring. She was in bird "sound heaven" listening to all the different phone rings. She especially liked the fax ring, no doubt because it wasn't a boring single beep, and, maybe more importantly, because it was different. I have noticed that new things, whether a sound or an object, get the bird's attention. Through the years, Richard and I always have kept the bird busy with new, interesting things to look at, play with, and listen to. After a little practice, Jayson mimicked the double fax ring so convincingly that even I had to listen carefully to determine whether it was a fax or the bird. Once in a while, she fooled even me. I would walk all the way upstairs to pick up a fax that never came in. I wonder if Jayson knew...

Jayson also likes other ringing or beeping machines, too, like the alarm clock. As with the fax, the bird is so adept she actually sounds like the beeping alarm. Probably because it was a more distant sound – and usually shut off within seconds of starting – Jayson mimicked the alarm only every so often, at least as far as I can tell, although she did beep with it only a few weeks ago, to my surprise (and delight...). I suppose I could have missed her beeping many times because the clock was so close to my ear. I'm just glad Jayson didn't figure out that beeping like the alarm clock on her own probably would wake me up...

A Little Fresh Air?

One day, in the middle of a business call that I had placed from the kitchen, Jayson began squawking intensely, the usual "jay-jay," "jay-jay" alarm call. She was reacting to an unfamiliar animal in the backyard. The squawk was loud enough to warn every blue jay within a half mile of the house, maybe further. The customer on the phone remarked that he just heard a loud blue jay, and without really thinking I blurted out "Oh, my office window is open. There's a noisy jay outside." The person on the phone simply accepted this explanation, which, after all, was quite plausible.

From that point on, whenever Jayson made any noise, other than her ringing, I used the "open window" explanation – it became an automatic response. I thought it was an excellent strategy and was a bit smug about it, even though I came upon it quite by accident. This strategy worked beautifully – until one day while I happened to be on the phone with a customer who asked if we were getting a lot of snow. I replied that we were "in the middle of a blizzard," which we were. No sooner had these words parted my lips, Jayson began squawking mightily in the background... Well, there went my "strategy"... After this embarrassing episode – I had to explain Jayson's entire story – I learned my lesson. From that day on I simply placed all business calls from my office, with the door tightly closed.

Jayson didn't confine her telephone games to the business phone. She also rang with our house phone, but the consequences were quite different. Some callers knew Jayson personally, for example, family and friends who had met her. When they called, upon hearing the bird in the background, most of them would chuckle and ask how she was doing. Jayson always evokes that sort of response. Everyone who knows the bird likes her and is curious and concerned about how she's doing.

Other callers had heard about the bird, but had never met her, for example, some of our kids' friends or especially their parents. Many of them heard Jayson on the phone for the first time. If the bird were squawking, invariably the reaction would be something like "Oh, that's the blue jay I've heard about." Believe me, a lot of very lengthy conversations began with that simple remark... If she were ringing, some would ask if I had to take that call, and, of course, I would tell them about the bird.

Naturally, there were many people who called and knew nothing at all about the bird. These were usually the most interesting phone calls. Just as with my business customers, some callers – most, in fact – asked about the blue jay noise in the background if she squawked and usually said nothing if she rang. But if the bird piped up, whether or not I was asked about her and whatever noise she made, I usually volunteered an explanation. It got to the point that I enjoyed telling people about Jayson. Even complete strangers were fascinated to hear her story. Through the years I have learned that telling it helps develop an awareness and appreciation of just how sophisticated blue jays are. Most people know very little about jays, and they're quite impressed when I tell them about Jayson's behaviors and intelligence.

- - - - - - - - - -

7

"Chitty Chitty Bang Bang"

— *The Song and the Movie*

"Also musical 'weedle weedle', like the squeaking of a farm pump that needs oil. Variety of other vocalizations, some musical."

— *Birds of New England*

It's hard to imagine that a bird watches television and pays attention to it, but Jayson does. It's also hard to imagine that a bird can learn and remember complex pieces of classical music, but Jayson does that, too.

The blue jay's vocalization is not limited to mimicking only short duration sounds, like animal noises or telephone rings. Blue jays also can learn complicated and long songs, and Jayson became very skilled at doing exactly this. Jayson lives in a very interesting world when it comes to sounds, and she took full advantage of it.

Needless to say, with five kids between seven and sixteen when Jayson showed up in 1984, our house was never quiet. For many years, something was always playing – the radio (often more than one), the stereo, the television, or the piano. There also were all sorts of other noises that occur in a busy house – noises the kids made, noises the dogs made, noises my husband and I made going about our own activities. Maybe because she was in the kitchen, Jayson really seemed to enjoy kitchen sounds, like pots clanging, the whirring food processor, or appliances that beeped.

Piano Duets

Jayson's reaction to sounds is very complex. There is no obvious or simple explanation why some sounds appeal to the bird so much more than others, at least not in any detailed way that I can fathom. But, after observing Jayson for many years, it is clear to me that there are a couple of important factors. One is melody. Sounds that are melodic – not necessarily songs – invariably interest the bird. Another is volume. Loud sounds get Jayson's attention, and she is much more likely to react to them than to quieter ones. There appears to be a balance between these factors.

Louder sounds that are not particularly melodic seem to get as much attention as quieter ones that are very melodic. An example of this balance was Jayson's reaction to the piano, which she listened to quite often.

One of my sons is an accomplished classical pianist. He loves to play and for many years practiced every day. When Jayson lived in the sunroom in our first house, the piano was three rooms away. While she could hear the piano, it was only a background sound at her cage. But when Jayson was relocated from the atrium into the kitchen in the new house, the piano was around the corner in the living room, which was connected to the kitchen by a wide opening. Now the piano was less than twenty feet away. Jayson couldn't see the piano, but she certainly heard it. Whenever my son played, the bird heard him playing, usually practicing cords and technique. These exercises were not especially loud or melodic, and Jayson showed no particular interest. But soon that changed.

Every piano student plays recitals, and my son was no exception. For one recital, he was assigned a Chopin *Polonaise* as his performance piece. When a piece is learned, the first thing the pianist does is "finger" the music so that playing it becomes second nature, pretty much memorizing the entire piece. This is a halting and arduous process for complicated classical pieces, neither loud nor melodic. As far as I could tell, Jayson paid no attention while my son fingered the *Polonaise*. She just went about her business – the bird is constantly moving – as if no one were playing a piano nearby.

Once the fingering is mastered, practicing the performance comes next. The pianist plays the piece over and over and over again, until it is mastered so thoroughly that it can be performed for an audience. My son spent weeks working on the *Polonaise*, and as a result, Jayson had been listening to it all that time. For most of this time, the bird did nothing – until one day she began to mimic the music and literally "played along" – for the entire piece! Jayson's performance was nothing short of spectacular, almost as if she had been practicing, too, and decided that she finally was ready for an audience.

The bird actually sang the melody that my son played, getting louder when he played louder, and softer when he played softer. What amazed me most was that Jayson really did follow the music. Listening to the bird gave the impression that she had memorized the score, her accompaniment was that faithful. Of course, I have no way of knowing for sure that Jayson actually memorized the score. But knowing the talented little bird as I do, it wouldn't surprise me in the least.

For a tiny creature, Jayson certainly can belt out a tune – she can make a *lot* of noise. When she sang along, there were times Jayson was so loud that my son couldn't concentrate on the music, to the point where he would stop playing, go over to the cage, and tell the bird to pipe down. Jayson did stop singing, but, of course, not because she was asked to. It was only because the music had stopped – the bird never sang the *Polonaise* alone. She insisted on piano accompaniment.

Jayson did to my son with the piano what she had done to me with the phone. Instead of ringing, she was singing. By any measure, what the bird did was incredible. But soon the novelty wore off. My son had a recital to get through, so he forced himself to ignore the bird – there was no way Jayson would stop singing along whenever he played. She obviously liked the *Polonaise* a lot, and had a wonderful time performing it, but only as the second "musician" in a duet. I think Jayson is one of my son's biggest fans. When recital day finally arrived, my son's performance was flawless.

Richard and I couldn't help but chuckle about what it took for him to get there...

How About a Movie?

One of my youngest daughter's favorite movies was *Chitty Chitty Bang Bang*. She would have watched it over and over again if I let her. Watching that movie, or any number of other movies, was a special treat. Richard and I, and the other kids, too, if they were around, would all sit down with popcorn and take in the flick. What I didn't realize was that our little feathered friend was watching, too.

After Jayson's cage was relocated from the atrium to the kitchen in the new house, she had a perfect view of the television. But we couldn't see her. The TV itself was about twenty feet away from the bird, in the family room. The couches we sat on to watch TV were on the opposite walls, so that Jayson's cage was obscured from our view. The bird was able to see everything on the screen, but we had no idea that she actually was watching. As it happens, Jayson not only watched TV, but it appears that she studied the *Chitty Chitty* movie as if it were a homework assignment.

One day when *Chitty Chitty* was playing, we thought we heard Jayson singing in the background. To find out, I turned down the volume and asked everyone to be quiet. Jayson stopped singing. I turned the volume back up, and, once again, we thought we heard the bird. Living with Jayson for all these years has taught me one thing for sure – that all of us had to invent clever ways of dealing with the bird's idiosyncrasies. On this day it was figuring out a way of determining whether or not she was singing. I outsmarted Jayson by lowering the volume somewhat, but not shutting it off entirely. The bird kept on singing, and what she was singing was the song *Chitty Chitty Bang Bang!*

The bird wasn't singing the words, of course – she sang the tune. As usual, the little bird was full of surprises. This time it was not only that she vocalized every note, but that she got the syncopation right. In this regard *Chitty Chitty* is a rather complex song, and Jayson's command of it was quite impressive. My guess is that Jayson studied the song because she liked it – the melody appealed to her. I suspect that she "practiced" for some time before actually belting out the tune. It would have been very easy for her to sing along quietly without our noticing, and I am sure that's just what she did.

"Sing Along with Mitch"

— 1960s TV Series

It's too bad that Jayson wasn't around during the heyday of the "sing along" show. I can only imagine how she would react to a TV show that actually wanted the audience to sing along. There's no doubt in my mind that Jayson would have been one of the loudest and best singers, and that she would have thoroughly enjoyed herself. I suppose Mitch Miller's bouncing ball probably would have had her bobbing, too...

After the *Chitty Chitty* incident, all of us noticed that Jayson sang selectively with tunes she liked, some from TV, some from the radio or the stereo, but most often from the piano. Maybe she was getting used to her new environment, because soon enough the bird began to sing more regularly, even when we were in the same room (but she never sang *her own* compositions unless she was alone). Exactly what there was about a particular song that she liked is anybody's guess. But there is no doubt that the bird was fussy about her music.

Jayson did pick and choose from all the songs she heard. And she sang along only with those she liked, usually rather quietly, but not always. It was quite humorous watching the bird crescendo with my son as he played the piano. Jayson would get louder and louder as the piano did, all in perfect time with the music. Sometimes the bird became theatrical, too. When she increased her volume, she actually would puff up, like a tenor singing opera.

Singing and Ringing

Another funny incident occurred one day when my son was playing the piano. He began to play louder and faster, and Jayson was merrily singing right along, keeping up with the volume and the tempo. While this was happening, the phone rang. Jayson's immediate reaction was to stop singing and start ringing – and, of course, bobbing. My son and I burst into laughter. He couldn't continue playing, and I couldn't answer the phone.

My memories of Jayson's singing are some of my fondest and most humorous. The bird sang up a storm for more than ten years, but then, as she aged, began to sing less and less. Now, at age twenty, she doesn't sing at all. She gradually stopped singing her own songs and singing along, even to tunes I know she liked. She still vocalizes quite a bit, chirping and squawking "jay-jay," and she still does some imitations. The one she likes the

Jayson enjoying sunning herself on a warm late fall day in her traveling cage on the deck, and having a grand old time squawking back at other birds. November 1997.

most, I'm quite sure, is her duck imitation. It was one of her first, and it seems still to be her favorite. But, sadly, Jayson's singing days are over, and I do miss them.

- - - - - - - - - -

8

Junk Food Junkie

*"Jays eat almost anything but prefer vegetable food,
especially tree seeds, which are often buried
for later consumption."*

— *North American Birdfeeder Handbook*

Blue jays like fruits and vegetables –
at least the jays that live outside do. Jayson doesn't
like either. She is a very unusual bird when it
comes to her eating habits. Getting her to eat fruits
and veggies is like trying to get the reluctant five
year old to eat Brussels sprouts or broccoli, almost
always a losing battle.

I suspect that most people would think of an
"acquired taste" principally as being a human trait.
Of course, animals also have acquired tastes, but
always for foods *not* in their natural diet. The dog
or cat that develops a taste for table food is a good

example. The essential notion of acquired taste is that it's one that Nature does not provide. By this definition, most of Jayson's tastes are "acquired."

Finicky, Finicky

In many ways Jayson's food preferences are exactly backwards from what they should be. Jayson really is "cut from a different mold," and the question, of course, is why. I think I know the answer. Whoever removed Jayson from her nest deprived her of learning eating habits from the mother blue jay. Jayson's food preferences strongly suggest that they are not instinctual. I now believe that a bird's eating habits are mostly learned from the mother bird. Whatever a chick is fed is what the chick develops a taste for.   Jayson ate mostly "people food" as a chick, and as a result she never developed a taste for a normal blue jay diet.

When we first got Jayson, one of the things I quickly noticed about her eating behavior was that she acted like a chick, not an adult bird. It was impossible not to notice, because in the beginning I fed her many times each day.   Whenever I approached with food, she would "open wide," emitting a plaintive chirp to get my attention. Jayson obviously did not realize that there was no competition, so she behaved as if there were other chicks squawking for each tasty morsel.

This behavior persisted for the entire time Jayson was fed her special diet of dog food, turkey starter, and the vitamin/mineral supplement. It probably was during that period as a chick that she could have developed a taste for fruits and vegetables. But these foods were not on the menu because the special diet was more important, hopefully to deal with her bone problems. So, as a chick, Jayson never developed a taste for what is supposed to be a major component of a blue jay's normal diet – fruits and veggies.

A Splash of Color

Not long after being weaned from being fed by me, Jayson's doctor told us she could eat whatever she wanted, as long as she also had her dog food twice a day. It was interesting to let the bird sample new foods, and I tried introducing her to a variety of them. I started with the ones the bird guides suggested a jay would want, especially fruits and berries, figuring that the bird would instinctively eat them. But, even though I tried every berry I could find, Jayson simply did not like them. Some of my attempts turned out to be quite funny. Jayson always had a good time making a mess whenever I gave her berries, especially colorful, juicy ones like strawberries, blueberries, raspberries, or blackberries.

She sampled the berry by nibbling a small piece using the very tip of her beak. Even though it didn't close, Jayson's beak was quite sharp, the perfect tool for breaking off the tiniest piece before eating any more. When it came to berries, she always would spit out the sample piece, and then smash the rest of the berry with her beak. This was great fun for the bird. She always had a good time dragging the smashed berry all over the foam rubber in her cage, leaving as she went colorful streaks of red, blue, pink, or purple. It didn't take me long to learn to let her try only one berry at a time...

Because I knew that blue jays are supposed to like berries, I naively thought that trying again and again would eventually wear down the bird. Sooner or later Jayson would wake up to the wonderful taste of fresh berries. Well, that never happened. Still, it was several years before I gave up entirely. Every so often I would try "one last time," hoping the bird would change her mind. To this day she has not.

Jayson sitting on her corner shelf. This photo provides a good view of the tip of her beak showing how it does not close.

Moving Food Around

Even though it was clear that Jayson hated berries – any berry as far as I can tell – I did try to introduce other fruits, hopefully some that would appeal to her. I think I have tried every available fruit, including melons (both cantaloupe and honey dew, for variety), pineapples, grapes, pears, peaches, apples, tomatoes, and on, and on, basically any fruit I had around the house. But whenever I gave the bird a piece of fruit, the result always was the same. She has been remarkably consistent through the years.

Jayson samples whatever fruit I give her using the same technique she developed for the berries. Then, invariably she spits out the fruit, and, depending on what it is, plays with it. Jayson treats cherries the way she does berries, smashing them and wiping the pieces on her foam to leave marks. Color matters a lot to the bird. After spitting out a fruit with clear juice, like an apple, Jayson simply ignores it, no wiping the foam, no playing. She likes to "paint" only with colorful berries.

Bananas are somewhere in between cherries and apples. They really don't have juice, but there is something about them that Jayson likes. Even though she doesn't eat bananas, she likes to play with them by moving banana pieces around her cage. She drops them here and there, then goes back, picks them up, and starts all over again. Interestingly, she doesn't bury bananas, because burying is reserved for food she likes. If Jayson doesn't like a food, she "moves it around the plate" without eating it, much as a child might.

Eat Your Vegetables!

When it comes to vegetables, the bird is almost as bad as she is with fruit. Jayson will not eat veggies, with exactly two exceptions – peas and corn.   The fact is, she actually likes these two vegetables, and even "begs" for one of them.   If Jayson sees peas on the table, she bounces around her cage, chirping until she gets my attention and I bring her some peas. A few peas are all it takes to make her a very happy little bird – she gobbles them up. If there happen to be any left, she buries them under her foam for a snack later on. Jayson doesn't beg for corn, but she loves it when I give it to her. Usually I give her a small piece of corn on the cob, and it's both a meal and a toy. Jayson plays with the corncob while she pulls off individual kernels to eat. But that's it for Jayson's veggies – corn and peas, nothing else.

Check Out the Buffet

Jayson's basic diet for twenty years has been dog food. Every day, twice a day, she receives a fresh platter of dog food, which she does eat. It was during the first return visit to the wildlife clinic that Jayson's doctor told us we could feed her pretty much anything she liked, because jays are omnivores. The only requirement was that her core diet remain the dog food to provide balanced nutrition. What this meant for the bird was a gastronomic adventure that continues to this day.

She likes to try new and different things, and we enjoy giving them to her.

Jayson "checking out the buffet." October 2000.

When her cage was moved from the atrium into the kitchen in the new house, Jayson had a bird's eye view of what was on the table at every meal. She scrutinized the entire table, and could identify foods she liked, and ones that were new. It is quite amazing that the bird recognizes certain foods from memory. There is no doubt that this is exactly what she does. Another intriguing behavior is that she lets me know she's watching, and that I should bring her a bite to eat.

Jayson usually is bouncing around her cage at the beginning of a meal. Now that she lives on the Cape, she is mostly at the back because that part of the cage looks outdoors. But wherever she is, and whatever she is doing, as soon as people sit at the table the bird moves to the front and becomes very still. She sits quietly in the front corner, checking out what is on the table. That the bird actually is doing this becomes obvious to anyone who carefully observes her.

If there is a food she likes that she wants me to bring to her, Jayson begins "muttering," chirping ever so softly under her breath. Muttering is the only way I can describe what she does, because, as odd as it may sound, it is reminiscent of a person muttering. The bird is so discrete in this behavior that most people, even family members, do not notice it. She stops muttering as soon as I stand, and immediately begins flapping and chirping louder. She knows something yummy is on the way, and gets excited in anticipation.

What's for Breakfast?

There is no doubt in my mind that Jayson's favorite meal is breakfast – not hers, but *ours*. The very first thing I do each day, after turning on the coffee pot, is feed Jayson. Her breakfast comes before ours, and she's usually wolfing it down before we sit. As soon as we sit down, as with every meal, the bird checks out the table, scouring it for something she likes. Over the years, she has developed very specific preferences in breakfast foods.

When Jayson sees something at breakfast that she wants, the "muttering" starts. She doesn't stop until I give her something. Her favorites, more or less in order, are pancakes with real maple syrup, toasted bagels with cream cheese, scrambled eggs, and, what can I say, cheerios. The cheerios are particularly interesting because they are both toys and a snack for the bird. Jayson enjoys picking up a bunch of cheerios by poking her beak through the hole – it's a very funny sight.

Good Eats

Jayson is an omnivore, but my husband jokingly calls her a "cannibal." His reason is that Jayson really likes meat. Her favorites are chicken and turkey. Naturally, this always comes up at Thanksgiving, and provides for plenty of humorous remarks as we make up a dish for the bird. Of course, on Thanksgiving Day the bird must eat Thanksgiving dinner with everyone else, which has been our ritual every year since 1984. It's Jayson's holiday, too, and she is very much a part of the family. I can tell that Jayson really enjoys the flurry of activity, all the hoopla and the people that she sees only occasionally, and, maybe more than anything else, the "good eats."

Holidays at my house are crowded, noisy affairs. Before dinner plenty of people mill around making conversation and munching on appetizers. The standard ones are always there, cheese and crackers, veggies and dip, salsa and tortillas, along with others I make or the kids bring. Jayson surveys the offerings and gets more than her share of "cookies" as people walking by the cage invariably give the bird a bite. But she never fills up on appetizers. Jayson always seems to have room for the main course, especially when it's a turkey dinner.

Jayson's meal includes a little of everything on our Thanksgiving menu: turkey with cranberry sauce, of course; and the "fixins," usually stuffing, sweet and mashed potatoes, and peas. I make sure there are peas at every Thanksgiving dinner, because the bird really likes them (they're not big with my kids...). There are other vegetables, too, but, true to form, Jayson will have none of them.

I always include the cranberry sauce in Jayson's plate, because, after all, it is Thanksgiving. What's turkey without cranberry sauce? But there is another reason, too. Even after all these years, a little part of me still hopes that Jayson might change her mind about berries. But, no, what the bird does is eat everything in the dish, especially the turkey, but never the cranberries...

A couple of hours after the main course, everyone sits for dessert. There are always plenty of them, usually too many – cakes, and cookies, and pies, and fruits, and nuts... These are all arranged in the center of the table, much to Jayson's delight. The bird absolutely has a sweet tooth, but, interestingly, still avoids the fruit pies. Blueberry pie, cherry pie, apple pie – none of these interests the bird in the least. But she loves cake, especially with ice cream. She loves cookies, any kind of cookie. And, even though they are not sweet,

Jayson loves nuts. She does have preferences, though, when it comes to nuts. Some she eats immediately, especially walnuts and peanuts, while others she plays with and eventually eats.

Thanksgiving probably is Jayson's favorite holiday. But there are many other occasions throughout the year when the bird has a similar good time – other holidays, birthday parties, graduations, whenever there's a crowd and food around. Jayson always is in the middle of a good time, chirping and bouncing around her cage, checking out the guests and what they're eating, and, of course, begging for her share – which she always gets.

Snakes and Meatballs!?

Another of Jayson's favorite meals is spaghetti and meatballs, with Italian bread no less. Spaghetti and meatballs is one of the foods that she readily recognizes and insists on being fed whenever we have it for dinner. While the bird loves all sorts of grains, there is no question that pasta is her favorite. But developing a taste for the spaghetti did not come easily. The first time I gave her a piece, Jayson recoiled – she squawked loudly, her alarm squawk, and immediately flew to the highest perch in her cage. She obviously was very scared.

I think Jayson thought the strand of spaghetti was a snake. Her reaction to it was so immediate and so intense, all I can imagine is that it was an instinctive fear of snakes. Eventually I got her to try the spaghetti by breaking the strand into small pieces. And from then on she was hooked – she loves pasta. These days, Jayson gets a full size piece of spaghetti, which she both eats and plays with. Maybe now that she is used to it, the spaghetti reminds her more of the worms she occasionally had as a chick (Richard would send out our youngest daughter to dig them up...), instead of a scary snake.

Feeding Jayson meatballs is the only way I can get any tomato into the bird (I still try to give her fruits...). She actually likes the tomato sauce, more so on the meatball than on the spaghetti. Even if the meatball is dripping with sauce, the bird gobbles it up. To the bird, pasta sauce and raw tomato are different enough that she will eat the tomato sauce, but not an uncooked tomato. Her reaction to the first piece of meatball I gave her was quite different than it was to the spaghetti. She immediately took it from me, not even hesitating as sometimes she does, tasted it, and wolfed it down. I

110

suspect she took it so quickly because the texture and appearance may be similar enough to her dog food's. Who knows, maybe Jayson thinks of meatball as a particularly tasty form of dog food. Meatballs and spaghetti, and other pastas, too, have become a staple in Jayson's diet. She enjoys eating them, and I enjoy feeding them to her.

Jayson Want a Cookie?

"Cookie" is one of the first words Jayson learned after learning her name. It has become a generic term for the bird, although it started out referring to real cookies. After the vet removed Jayson's dietary restrictions, we naturally experimented with all sorts of foods to see what she liked. Cookies were among them. As it turns out, Jayson loves cookies so much that when anyone says "Jayson want a cookie?", she reacts by flapping, chirping, and immediately coming to the front of the cage to collect her prize.

She gently takes the cookie out of your hand, as long as she knows and likes you. Because her reaction was so strong and predictable, Jayson was summoned with "want a cookie" even if she were offered something else, say, a potato chip. The bird now associates "cookie" with junk food, and she loves all of it. Popcorn, potato chips, pretzels, corn chips, and crackers, for example, are now among Jayson's favorite foods. She demands her share if she sees anyone else eating them. The little bird is very successful at getting people to give her what she wants. Jayson is so hooked on junk food that she actually will spit out other food if she sees someone walk by with a chip or something else she likes, a ploy that works just about every time. Over the years, Jayson certainly has lived up to being an "omnivore," especially when it comes to her acquired taste for junk food...

- - - - - - - - - -

9

Crickets & Moths & Flies, Oh My!

"It eats many insects and is one of the few avian predators on hairy caterpillars."
— *Song and Garden Birds of North America*

Blue jays like seeds and bugs, and Jayson does, too. Finally there was a "natural" food that Jayson liked! Of course, I will never know for sure how she developed a taste for seeds and bugs, but I do have some ideas. In keeping with my theory that birds learn dietary preferences from the mother bird, I suspect that whoever took Jayson from her nest probably fed her seeds and bugs. These are foods that most people intuitively would expect a bird to eat, whereas fruits and vegetables are much less intuitive. Even if this hypothesis is not correct, the fortunate result is that Jayson has always liked seeds and bugs, which are good for her.

For a Rainy Day

Seeds are a reliable staple in Jayson's diet, and they are very important. Unlike most other foods, especially meats, seeds do not deteriorate quickly, so that the bird has a nutritious meal whenever she needs it. Jayson is never left alone for too long, but occasionally we have to be away overnight. Doing this would be impossible without leaving her seeds. I make sure she has a variety of seeds, both because she prefers certain kinds, and also because she is constantly busy playing with them.

I fed the birds outside long before becoming Jayson's adopted mom, and I still do. I learned early on that birds have strong preferences for certain types of seed. For example, the outside jays never eat thistle, but they do like suet and sunflower seeds. The small songbirds, like finches, enjoy the thistle. Jayson is finicky, too, up to a point. She won't eat thistle, and she definitely likes sunflower seeds. She also seems to like a variety of other seeds, but not as much. To keep her happy, Jayson's cage always has at least one seed dish filled with a wild bird mix. It includes many different seed types, and Jayson is quite picky about which ones she eats. The bird is busy for hours on end sorting, playing with, burying, and eating her seeds.

Jayson gulping down seeds. June 1985.

Jayson has developed what I believe is her own, unique sorting scheme for finding just the seeds she likes and wants. She approaches her seed dish, looks it over in minute detail, tilting her head from side to side to improve the view, then uses her beak to scatter seed all over the cage – and the kitchen floor, too... Jayson literally launches the seeds out of the dish by swiping her beak back and forth. It sounds a lot like a maraca, and I am sure she gets a big kick out of making the noise while scattering the seeds. Not only do the seeds end up on the kitchen floor, but also in the potted plants below her cage. Every so often I see something growing in one of the pots that shouldn't be there. And, of course, I know where it came from...

When enough seed is strewn around the cage, the bird goes into "hunting" mode. She bounces from seed to seed, one at a time, inspecting each one, eating some on the spot, ignoring others, and burying certain select ones, either in the foam rubber or under it. At any given time, Jayson must have enough buried seeds to feed herself for a week.

Sunflower seeds are, or were, Jayson's favorite. She would pick up a seed, hold it firmly with her feet, and "power peck" until it broke open. She then ate the meat, and grabbed another seed. Jayson would do this off and on all day long, taking breaks to play with something else when she got bored. Eventually she was full from eating seeds, but that only gave her a reason to bury them. If she ran out of sunflower seeds, she would dig up the ones cached in her cage, and either eat them or relocate them to a better spot.

Jayson had a good time managing her seed supply, and this activity accounted for a large part of the day, when she was able to do it. As Jayson has aged, her feet have deteriorated to the point where now she is unable to open a sunflower seed. Our solution to this problem is to give her shelled sunflower seeds mixed in with her other seeds. These may not be quite as much fun for Jayson, but she really seems to enjoy eating and burying them.

Jayson also likes nuts. She has a passion for walnuts and peanuts. Her absolute favorite is walnuts – shelled, of course. I make a point of having walnuts in the pantry as a special treat for the bird. Peanuts, on the other hand, I do not keep around – because I will eat them. In fact, I like peanuts so much, that I might fight the bird for them...

On special occasions when there are peanuts or mixed nuts around, Jayson demands her share from anyone who happens to walk by with nuts in hand. She squawks and bounces around until she gets that person's attention and is fed a nut. Jayson is very persistent, and consequently very successful. People who don't know the bird well find this behavior quite fascinating, and, of course, are happy to give her a tidbit.

Butch to the Rescue

Bugs are an excellent source of protein, at least that is what I have heard. I wonder if they taste like chicken? Jayson likes bugs, not all bugs, but many bugs. I must admit, at first I didn't think to get her bugs, but serendipity worked once more in Jayson's favor. It happened when Butch the lizard showed up in 1987, three years after Jayson arrived.

One day the phone rang, and the caller identified himself as the owner of the pet shop where I bought Annabelle (the "Beast"). Through the years we had developed a casual friendship because I would buy my pet supplies at his store. He frequently asked about the dog, and years later still joked about the time she got loose. He told me he was calling because one of my kids, my daughter who was sixteen ay the time, was in the store looking to buy a lizard. I thought this was very curious, because this girl had no fondness for reptiles of any kind. I had no clue that she was off to the pet store, so I asked to speak to her.

My daughter explained that she wanted to buy her brother a birthday present, and that she knew he would really like a lizard for a pet. We used to keep fish, but at the time did not have a functioning aquarium. We did have a couple of tanks in the attic and most of the paraphernalia to set up a terrarium. My daughter told me that the store owner refused to sell her the lizard – she wasn't old enough. She had to be eighteen to buy an animal from the store. She pleaded with me to talk to the store owner, to tell him it was okay for her to buy the lizard.

I asked several questions about the lizard, which she described as being about six inches long and "kind of cute." When I asked about accommodations, she explained that, according to the store owner, one of the unused fish tanks would be a perfect house for the lizard. Finally I asked about feeding the lizard, what do lizards eat? She talked to the store owner, and relayed his reply – "lizard food." Hearing this, after briefly thinking about it, I told her buying the lizard was fine. I suppose I should have paid more attention, because I thought lizard food, like fish food, would be a flaky mixture that comes in a shaker dispenser... A while later, my daughter came home with her brother's birthday present in a small box with air holes. In her other hand was a small, brown paper bag. And on her face was a sheepish grin. I knew something was up, and I asked her if everything was all right. She reassured me and said she wanted to go wrap her brother's gift.

After dinner that night we celebrated my second oldest son's birthday with cake and ice cream, and, of course, birthday presents. My daughter gave him the lizard camouflaged in a big box that contained the little one and the brown paper bag. My son was absolutely delighted when he saw the lizard. It was "the best," "way cool," and other teenager superlatives. Then he opened the paper bag to see what was inside, and much to everyone's surprise, especially mine, a live cricket jumped out. It wasn't a black cricket, the kind you see in the grass – it was a brownish-gray color. At first I thought it was some sort of roach. I was horrified.

Of course, Jayson's take on things was quite different. I was not paying attention to the bird when this happened, but the bird certainly was paying attention to us. As she usually did, Jayson was sitting quietly in her cage checking out what was for dessert. Cake and ice cream are high on her list of desirable desserts. But when she saw the cricket, the bird discovered the best dessert. While Jayson got all worked up about what she thought of as a scrumptious morsel, I was thoroughly disgusted by this bug walking around my table.

My immediate reaction was that the lizard had to go, not because of the lizard itself, but instead because of the "lizard food." I was hoodwinked, both by my daughter and by my "friend," the pet store owner. I would have thought he owed me a favor for taking Annabelle off his hands, but I guess not. So he got a call from me about the "lizard food"... He laughed, admitting that he had hoodwinked me, and explained that he knew I never would agree to the lizard if he told me what they eat. To his credit, he was nice enough to offer to take the lizard back. But, of course, in the end, the lizard stayed, and my son set up a very attractive terrarium. He named the lizard Butch, who lived quietly in his terrarium, surrounded by breakfast, lunch and dinner – all the live crickets. I frequently saw a cricket sitting on Butch's head, sometimes for quite a while... until Butch got hungry... The crickets turned out not to be a problem because they were enclosed in Butch's terrarium, and I had nothing to do with them.

Butch's arrival was a bonanza for Jayson. She now had a source of fresh, tasty crickets. Before giving the bird her first cricket, I checked with the wildlife clinic, just to be sure. I was told she could eat any bug she liked. Watching the bird eat a cricket is not a pretty sight, but it is the natural order of things. And, most importantly, Jayson loved them!

Lizards Need Variety, too

And our scaly friend Butch was no exception. While crickets were the mainstay of his diet, he also liked a variety of other foods. Lettuce and other vegetables were high on his list. Also high on the list were mealworms, the wormlike beetle larvae pet stores sell as, you guessed it, "lizard food." The problem with mealworms is that they're kept in the refrigerator, and even though the container was sealed *very* tightly, I never could get by the idea of having live bugs in my fridge.

Butch was with us for about four years, and all that time he ate crickets, and so did Jayson. The mealworms lasted a much shorter time – I don't recall exactly how long. What I can say for sure is that it was no longer than that first container lasted... As it turns out, Jayson really liked mealworms, but, since she's an omnivore, well, those little bugs are where I drew the line.

A Tasty "Mothful"

Seeing how much Jayson liked crickets, any bug now became fair game. Living in the woods provided an endless supply of tasty bugs, all kinds, especially during the warm summer months. Moths were especially easy to get. Hundreds of them swarmed around the lights at the back of the house, and it took only a few minutes to collect a bunch. That job fell to my husband, who then fed them to the bird. This was one of the few times Jayson seemed to like Richard.

Some moths were clearly tastier than others. Jayson really liked the little white ones. But the bigger moths, especially brown moths, were a different story. She liked some, but not most. The medium-sized, light brown ones were okay. But the big, furry, dark brown ones she did not like at all. If she were given one, she literally would spit it out, with the sort of look "yucky" tastes provoke.

Besides eating the moths, Jayson made sport of playing with them, picking them up and letting them go, and doing this a couple of times before gulping them down. She actually played with the moth in much the same way a cat plays with a mouse. While this was a fascinating display, I must admit I felt sorry for the moth, especially the cute little white ones, which happened to be Jayson's favorite. Even though the moths tried to escape, especially the larger ones, none ever made it. Jayson was far too quick and accurate, and in her younger days very much at the top of her game.

Here, Anty, Anty...

Living in the woods also provides easy access to ants, especially carpenter ants, the shiny black ones about three-quarters of an inch long that like to nest, of all places, in the timbers of your house. My husband hates carpenter ants... For the fourteen years we lived in our second house, Richard had a running battle with them. I think he managed to hold off the ants pretty much (you never can be sure...), but he never quite won the war. Carpenter ants also were a bit of a problem in our first house, but nothing like they were in the middle of the dense woods where our second house was located. The ants were everywhere, and besides crawling around, they swarm once or twice a year.

So, when Jayson's doctor told us that she could eat any bug she liked, I knew exactly why my husband smiled the way he did – Jayson was about to get a true gastronomic delight, carpenter ants, probably served up in more ways than you could imagine. I'm sure that if there were a book titled "101 Ways to Prepare Carpenter Ants," my husband would be reading it.

But there was a problem... Jayson didn't like to eat ants. She didn't like them at first, and she still doesn't (like me with berries, Richard kept trying for a long time with the ants...). It was only recently, by which I mean, oh, say, within the past ten years, that Richard figured out why. There is a very curious bird activity actually called "anting." Certain species of birds, jays especially, use ants to kill parasitic feather lice by rubbing the ant's body against their feathers. Apparently formic acid from the ant's body helps control the lice. Nature truly is fascinating, and this, I think, is a wonderful example. Of course, it also explains Jayson's behavior towards ants – they're her friends, not tasty tidbits, like a moth or a fly. In the wild, blue jays don't eat ants. Well, in captivity, they don't eat them either, much to my husband's chagrin...

S.W.A.T.

SWAT stands for "Special weapons and tactics," the kind used to apprehend especially dangerous criminals. Well, when it came to swatting flies, Jayson was a SWAT team all by herself. Her beak was the weapon, and her "bird brain" developed the tactics. If a fly happens to get in the house and the bird sees it, she tracks it like radar. Anyone who watches the bird closely will notice how she fixes on the fly, following its every movement, never losing track of where it is as long as she can see it. Fortunately for Jayson, flies, like crickets, are not too bright. The ones that make the fatal error in judgment of flying into Jayson's cage never come out – they very quickly become tasty tidbits for the little blue jay.

In her heyday Jayson was lightning fast, and never missed. Because she flew when she was young, a fly zooming overhead only made the chase more interesting. Jayson would calculate and fly an intercept course, snatching the intruder with her beak at exactly the right moment. This may sound dramatic – and it was. The bird was a deadly bug hunter. It is no surprise to me that wild jays are very successful in supplementing their diets with all the bugs they want. I cannot imagine a bug being able to elude a jay that's determined to make a meal of it.

The Buffet, Please

Jayson's acquired tastes are somewhat eclectic for a wild bird. She likes all sorts of foods that probably she shouldn't, and she is very picky about the natural foods she should like. The bird will not eat fruits, and likes only two veggies. But she does like grains and cereals, seeds and nuts.

During the twenty years I have cared for Jayson, one of the most interesting things has been experimenting with and trying to understand her dietary preferences.

The core concern always has been to give the bird the proper nutrition, and the fact that she has lived for twenty years I think shows that we got that right. Even now that the bird is quite old, I still like to give Jayson new foods, although after all these years there aren't many that the bird has not tried. The fact that Jayson is omnivorous helps a lot, because she is very cooperative in trying new foods.

These days, in her old age, the bird gets a fairly routine diet, because it is what has worked so well. She likes what we feed her, and the variety tends to keep her busy. Jayson is fed twice a day, early in the morning and again mid-afternoon (not counting all the snacks she gets). Her standard "variety platter" consists of dog food, ham, turkey, cheese, crushed walnuts, and several grains or cereals. She loves cheerios, but usually gets a couple of other cereals, too, like corn flakes, puffed wheat, oat bran, whatever happens to be in the pantry (none with sugar, though...).

When my grandkids visit, I put all of them to work in the morning making up Jayson's "gourmet" breakfast platter. The little kids get the biggest kick out of helping grandma by breaking the bird's food into small pieces and arranging it neatly in separate piles on Jayson's dish. After the platter

Jayson's "gourmet" breakfast platter, including (starting at the top, clockwise) ham, wheat chex, cherrios, puffed rice, dog food, turkey, shredded mozzarella cheese, and topping it all off, a "cookie".

is made, Richard holds each of the grandkids up for a short time to watch the bird eat. The little guys thoroughly enjoy this, to the point that they argue about who gets which food to prepare and who will be first to watch Jayson dig in. When they arrive for a visit, Jayson usually is mentioned as soon as they walk in, and they always ask about the bird during phone calls. The grandkids have learned a lot about birds and wildlife from our conversations about Jayson. The bird has made a profound mark on their lives, and I am glad my grandchildren have had a chance to get to know Jayson.

The grandkids help prepare Jayson's food dish, but I don't let them handle the bird's seed or water dishes (too messy...). Jayson always has a seed dish with a wild bird mix. And, of course, the bird always has plenty of water. Her morning water dish has vitamins in it, and the afternoon one usually is plain. The water always is served cold with ice cubes – Jayson not only prefers the water chilled, but occasionally she likes to play with the ice cubes. This diet has kept Jayson going for twenty years, and I hope it does for many years to come

Without doubt food is a central theme in Jayson's life, as I suppose it is with any animal. For Jayson food is both sustenance and, in a sense, her full-time "job." If she isn't nibbling, the bird is busy "managing" her food supply. Jayson picks at her food all day long, eating some, burying some, or just playing with it. Managing her food still plays a major role in how Jayson spends her time, and she seems to be quite happy doing it...

- - - - - - - - - -

10

Playing Dead

"Presented with new problems, [birds] appear to find the answers by a quick reorganization of their previous experience, without trials."

— *World of Birds*

Anyone who owns an animal probably has experienced the feeling of fright and panic when something bad happens. It might be a dog or cat running off and not coming home, or darting into a busy street, or eating something potentially harmful, or showing some extremely odd behavior. Because animals cannot explain what is happening, situations like these are very unsettling. In Jayson's case, I would have thought that her cage not only would keep the bird in, but also would keep these kinds of problems out. Of course, I was wrong.

Houdini

My heart was in my throat the day I saw Jayson sitting on the kitchen floor, and Abigail – the bird dog – was only a few steps behind me. I can hardly describe my sense of fright and panic as I imagined the dog catching and killing the bird. Fortunately I had the presence of mind to turn around and grab the dog's collar before she saw the bird. This happened one morning as I was coming downstairs. I calmly brought the dog back upstairs and locked her in a room. Thankfully, Jayson was spared.

Now I had to deal with the bird. My first concern was for Jayson's safety. I walked cautiously and quietly over to her, and, much to my surprise, she didn't fly off as I approached. She was standing very still in the middle of the kitchen floor, with an almost glassy stare. I didn't know why at the time, but some months later I would find out. The atrium ceiling was more than twenty feet high, and there was one plant that grew all the way up. If Jayson wanted to avoid going back into her cage, there was no way I could stop her. If she wanted to, the bird could have avoided capture for a very long time, maybe days.

I was quite surprised again when she allowed me to pick her up – she actually seemed to be happy that I did. My attention was focused entirely on the bird – I had not even looked at her cage. When finally I did, I was shocked to discover that the door to the cage was closed tight. I opened it and gently put Jayson back in. I carefully inspected the entire cage, especially the door. The door was held closed – "locked" – by tying two ribbons, one at the top, and one at the bottom. Jayson occasionally fidgeted with the bottom ribbon, but she couldn't reach the top one. I carefully looked over the cage. Both ribbons were tied, and there was nothing unusual. It was a real mystery to me how the bird got out. There was only one possible explanation – Jayson got out by squeezing through the bars. The problem with this theory was that she had been in this cage for several years and never before had gotten out.

Putting aside *how* Jayson got out, I now had to deal with the fact that she *did* get out. The dog posed a real threat to the bird, and it was my responsibility to keep the bird safe. There were two solutions to the problem. One was to build yet another cage, with closer spacing of the wooden dowels. Another was to add some type of barrier to the present cage. We chose the second, because building another cage would take some time, and

Jayson sitting in front of the rock in her corner cage decorated for Christmas. The photo shows the ribbons tying the door closed, and some toys (baby keys, bells), a cuttlebone, and a nest (just in case…). The flash reflection is from a Plexiglas panel. December 1994.

the situation required an immediate fix. I never again wanted to experience the fright that I had that morning. My husband solved the problem by custom-fitting Plexiglas panels around the entire perimeter of the cage. This made it impossible for Jayson to squeeze through the bars, and it worked perfectly.

A Bump on the Head

For several months after finding the bird on the kitchen floor, I thought Jayson was a birdie Houdini – that she squeezed herself through what seemed to be an impossibly small opening. But that is not what happened... One afternoon as I was going about my business in the kitchen, I heard a different flapping sound coming from the cage. I ran over to the cage to find the bird on her shelf, not really flapping, but instead twitching and flailing her wings uncontrollably.

Jayson was throwing her head back and forth violently, her mouth was opening and closing spastically, and her entire body quivered. Instinctively I knew the bird was having a seizure. She fell off her shelf onto the clean-out tray at the bottom of the cage. She landed hard, and continued to seizure. I thought my little bird was dying, and there was nothing I could do. Then, suddenly, to my immeasurable relief, the seizure stopped just as abruptly as it had started. I cannot describe how I felt when the seizure stopped. Watching it was horrible. Thankfully, this entire episode lasted less than a minute.

I regained my composure over the next several minutes as I watched Jayson recover. For a short time she kept rolling her eyes back, but soon that stopped, too, and she became more normal both in her appearance and her behavior. Jayson rested on the clean-out tray for some time, probably the better part of half an hour, looking somewhat dazed, or, should I say, "glassy eyed." I watched the bird intently, but I did not want to disturb her for fear of making things worse. I finally knew she was okay, at least for the time being, when she flew back up to her shelf. She started doing her usual things, pecking at her food and drinking some water.

While Jayson was sitting on the clean-out tray, I called the wildlife clinic and spoke directly to her veterinarian. I described everything that had happened and what the bird was doing while we were on the phone. The doctor's assessment was that the bird indeed had seizured, that she might continue to seizure, and that there wasn't much that could be done. It was impossible to know how often the bird would seizure. It might never happen again, or it could be sporadic, or quite frequent.

The doctor explained that the normal treatment would be an anti-seizure medication. But, in Jayson's case, dosing the bird would be very tricky. Jayson weighed between two and three ounces, and in such a small animal there was a very substantial risk that the medication could do more harm than good if she were given even slightly more than she could safely tolerate. The risk in so small a bird was too great. The doctor's advice to me was to watch the bird closely and report any subsequent events. If seizures became frequent, he wanted to see the bird...

As far as the bird's eyes rolling back was concerned, in the vet's opinion it likely was not due to the seizure. It probably resulted from the bump to her head when she fell. The doctor strongly advised that we close the gap between the shelves in Jayson's cage, so that she could not fall again. I called my husband and told him about these terrible events and what Jayson's doctor had said. Richard immediately came home early to start the cage modifications.

Jayson eventually was diagnosed as being epileptic, based on the fact that she did have other seizures. The mystery of how she had gotten out of her cage was solved a few months later when one day I observed her during a seizure. I am quite sure the day I found her on the kitchen floor, she had seizured and had gotten caught between the bars of the cage. In trying to get free, I suspect she wiggled through the bars, landing on the floor. It was a very good thing that we installed the Plexiglas panels, because otherwise the bird might have been seriously injured.

Following the doctor's orders, we replaced the two separate shelves in Jayson's cage with one main shelf consisting of separate pieces. The bird still had the corner shelf on the left about one foot above the main shelf, because at the time she was still flying and she regularly perched on it. To protect Jayson's feet, the main shelf now was covered by several pieces of foam rubber making it easier to replace and clean the foam. And the built-in tubby and water dish were still there, too. This arrangement prevented the bird from falling, except possibly from the corner shelf onto the main shelf. But since the main shelf now was covered with foam rubber, if the bird did fall, the possibility of a serious bump was eliminated. Unfortunately, the new setup also eliminated the clean-out tray, and the result was that I had to clean the cage several times a day, which I still do.

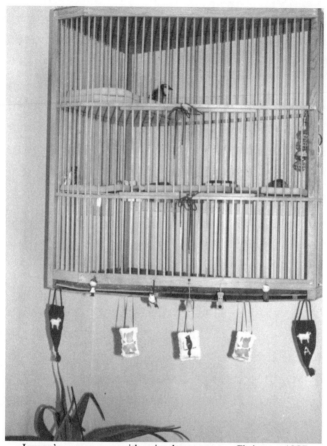
Jayson's corner cage with animal ornaments. Christmas 1997.

These events happened, as best I can recall, around 1991, more than thirteen years ago. Jayson has been epileptic ever since, and still seizures every so often.   I have consulted several veterinarians, and they all tell the same story – that there really isn't anything that can be done. In spite of her epilepsy, Jayson always seems to be very happy, and she recovers extremely quickly from a seizure episode. A seizure might last fifteen seconds, and as soon as it's over, the bird shakes her head, for some reason always wipes her beak on the foam, and then picks up something to eat. She does this every time, without fail. In between these sporadic episodes, the bird is perfectly normal.

Huffin' and Puffin'

One day I watched a very interesting television show on bird training. An expert trainer was talking about training birds of prey, specifically falcons. He had one of his students with him, and the bird did some very impressive stunts. The trainer said that before a bird could be trained, the trainer had to understand that birds don't like to fly. It's simply too much work, that is, unless the bird has a very good reason to fly, such as finding food, or heading south for the winter... At first I thought the bird expert's statement was nonsense. But after mulling it over, it actually made sense, and I felt better about Jayson's living in a cage, which at some level always bothered me. Of course, like any athlete – and birds are very athletic – not using muscles can result in rapid de-conditioning. That turned out to be the downside of Jayson's lifestyle, not lacking an opportunity to fly a lot, which presumably she wouldn't want to do anyway.

One day while I was in the middle of cleaning the bird's cage, the phone rang. In my rush to answer it (yes, Jayson was ringing, too…), I forgot to close the cage door. A couple of minutes later, when I was off the phone, I glanced at the cage to see the door open and the bird missing. Fortunately, as a precaution I had developed the habit of always putting Abigail outside when I worked on the birdcage (our dog Baron passed away in 1992). So I didn't have to worry about Abigail getting the bird – all I had to do now was find Jayson.

I looked around frantically, but didn't see her. My guess was that she was somewhere in the atrium, which was connected to the kitchen, or that she had flown upstairs. Sure 'enough, looking carefully around, there was Jayson sitting on one of the beams in the atrium looking down at me. I called to her thinking that maybe she would fly to me, but she didn't. In looking closely at the bird, she seemed nervous and stressed, and a few minutes later I believe I found out why.

Right at the moment, though, I was trying to think of ways to get to the bird as quickly as possible. But before I was able to do anything, Jayson decided to go for a spin around the atrium. She flew from the beam onto a tall yucca tree, twelve feet or so high, and from there onto another beam. The bird was squawking, visibly agitated, and seemed desperately to be looking for something. It's what she did next that really surprised me.

When Jayson saw her cage, she immediately made a beeline flying into it. I think the bird was disoriented in the atrium, and probably frightened. Back in her cage, she calmed right down. The poor little bird was obviously winded, literally huffing and puffing. This was the longest flight Jayson ever may have made, and she wasn't in the best shape to fly. The jays outside fly all the time, out of necessity. Jayson only flew around her cage recreationally – or maybe to catch a fly... When finally she calmed down, Jayson took a drink, nibbled on some food, and started bouncing around her cage. That is when I knew she was okay. It was clear that Jayson was very happy to be home. I believe that Jayson thinks of her cage as "home," and that she actually would be unhappy anywhere else.

Only Bats do That!

I have to relate this next anecdote second hand. It happened not to me, but to my husband, Richard, who told me the story. Of course, I have run this version by him, and he agrees it is accurate and complete. Even though in the morning I usually was downstairs before him, occasionally Richard went down before me. It was a good thing this particular day that he did (it is funny how some things just seem to "work out"…). Richard entered the kitchen, turned on the coffee pot, and was about to say good morning to the bird, when he looked over at the cage and was horrified at what he saw.

Jayson was hanging upside down from her corner shelf, motionless, with her wings spread out in the middle of the cage. My husband was completely shocked. He walked over to the cage and looked closely at Jayson. There was no sign of life, no sign whatsoever. She was absolutely, completely still, and her eyes were closed. One of her talons was caught in the edge of the foam rubber, so that the bird was hanging upside down like a bat with her wings extended.

Richard immediately concluded that Jayson probably had a stroke or heart attack during the night, and had fallen off the corner shelf as a result.

Her fall was broken when the talon got caught in the foam. Richard was completely choked up – he knew the bird was dead. After forcing himself to regain some measure of composure, his next concern was preventing me from seeing the bird this way. He thought I couldn't handle seeing Jayson hanging upside down from her corner shelf with her wings spread out – of course, he was right.

Over the next several minutes, my husband hatched a plan to minimize my trauma. He decided to very carefully remove the bird and place her gently on the foam in the middle of the main shelf. If necessary, he would keep her wings spread out, but he was hoping that he would be able to tuck them in, so the bird would look peaceful and natural. It took some doing for my husband to get up the courage to move the bird, but finally he did. All this time he was staring at the bird, and Jayson remained absolutely, completely still. There was no question – Jayson was gone.

Richard went over to the cage, pulled up a chair to stand on, opened the door, and reached in. When he touched the bird ever so slightly, he got the surprise of his life. Jayson's closed eyes suddenly opened wide, and she began to flail and squawk. She flapped around so much that she pulled her talon from the foam rubber, and fell onto the main shelf. She immediately righted herself and began bouncing around as if nothing at all had happened. She went to her water dish, took a drink, and started pecking at her seeds.

My husband's reaction was a lot like the audience's reaction in a scary movie – when a supposedly dead person suddenly opens their eyes and jumps up. Richard was so startled he had to catch his breath. Naturally, he was relieved and happy that Jayson actually was okay – but he got the fright of his life from what had happened.

I don't know how I would have reacted to this situation. Truth be told, I am glad it was my husband, not I. After the fact, of course, I can see there's a certain dark humor in this story, the way the bird "came back to life." You can imagine how happy I am that she did.

I also see this episode as yet another measure of Jayson's toughness and resilience. The little bird has been through an awful lot in her twenty years, from finding me to get help the day she hopped into my garage sopping wet, to undergoing surgeries, to dealing with hanging upside down for what might have been quite a while, and to dealing with many other problems. Jayson has managed to beat adversity every time.

The fact is, time and again, Jayson shows herself to be one feisty little blue jay...

- - - - - - - - - -

11

Bird Brain?

"Birds are creatures of instinct. ...and often are improved by experience, by learning; and the learning and memory abilities of birds can be marvelous."

— *World of Birds*

After living with Jayson all these years, I must say I wonder where the epithet "birdbrain" comes from. A birdbrain is someone not too bright. Jayson has a bird's brain, but she certainly isn't stupid. Observing her variety of behaviors, reactions, and interactions under all sorts of circumstances convinces me that the bird is actually quite intelligent by animal standards.

There's Mom & Dad!

We made every effort to avoid unnecessary trips to the wildlife clinic. Taking

146

Jayson out of her cage, putting her in the traveling cage, placing that cage in the car, and driving to the clinic, all this frazzled the bird. She became nervous and edgy, moving about quickly, sometimes frantically, and she made strange noises. The upset to her routine inevitably was distressing, and she let us know it. But, interestingly, she didn't squawk. I think at some level the bird still was comfortable, because she knew there was no great threat. She was, after all, in one of her houses, and we always were nearby to comfort her.

Unfortunately not all trips could be avoided. Most of Jayson's clinic visits were for routine checkups. Some were for emergencies. We always stayed during her routine checkups, but on one visit we could not. An emergency had come up at the clinic – the staff, including Jayson's veterinarian, had to perform emergency surgery on a fox. We were hurriedly told to leave the bird and come back later in the day.

We reluctantly left her, because coming back another day would require another trip, which would have been even worse for the bird. We put Jayson's cage on the floor in the hall near one of the exam rooms, said goodbye to her, and left. Later that afternoon we called and were told that Jayson was ready to be picked up. She had been given a physical, had her beak trimmed and her nails clipped, and, by the way, the fox was "resting comfortably."

A surprise came when we walked into the clinic to pick up the bird. Jayson saw us at the end of the hall, some twenty feet away, and immediately began chirping very loudly and flitting around the cage. She was so noisy that several of the clinic staff, including her doctor, came out to see what the fuss was about. Her vet looked at her, looked at us some distance down the hall, and was astonished at the bird's behavior.

He turned to his colleagues and explained how amazed he was that Jayson seemed not only to recognize us, but also to be genuinely happy to see us. Suddenly Jayson's behavior was completely different. All day long, the bird had been in a blue funk, sitting quietly and forlornly at the back of her cage. Now that "mom and dad" had come to pick her up, she was one happy little bird. Recognizing my husband and me, and reacting happily, apparently because she knew we were there to get her, I think is an example of how smart the bird really is. Her doctor and everyone else standing in the hall certainly were impressed.

Happiness is a State of Mind

I often wonder if Jayson is happy. It would be cruel to cage her if she were not, and that would break my heart. By any measure I can think of, Jayson seems to be a very happy little bird. This belief gives me comfort and helps me deal with her situation. Of course, I can only infer that she is happy from her behavior, but I do think this is a reasonable thing to do. Perhaps one of the best measures of Jayson's "state of mind" is the way she interacts with people, and how well she has settled into her life as a "kept" bird.

I think Jayson's intelligence has been a key factor in helping her adapt and feel comfortable in her domestic surroundings. Jayson truly has become a family member, in just the same way a pet dog or cat would. She knows us, and likes us. And everyone who meets the bird takes a liking to her, and, for most people anyway, the bird to them. Jayson recognizes people, and animals, by appearance and by sound. There are many interesting examples of this behavior.

In the morning, I would usually come downstairs before my husband, and Jayson always would greet me. I knew when Richard was walking down the stairs, which I could not see from the kitchen, because Jayson would tell me he was coming. I didn't hear a thing, but I am sure the bird did, or maybe she saw something I couldn't. She somehow knew that Richard was walking down the stairs, and she greeted him by chirping softy at first and getting louder and louder as he got to the bottom of the stairs.

Even though my husband and Jayson have a less friendly relationship than she does with me, she nevertheless is happy to see him, and shows that by her behavior. If other people, even people she knows and likes, stay overnight, Jayson does not react the same way. She might acknowledge their entering the room, but she certainly would not tell me they were walking down the stairs. Jayson is completely tuned into her environment – who and what is around her. The bird's reaction to Richard's coming downstairs is a good example of how Jayson pays attention to everything going on around her, and how she is selective in her response to certain situations.

Necessity, the Mother of Invention

And Jayson is quite inventive. She gets what she wants by figuring out ways of controlling some aspects of her environment. Because the bird is caged, she gets food only when people bring it to her, unlike a wild jay that forages freely. Jayson invented "muttering" to get my attention, so that I would bring her food when she wanted it.

I don't remember exactly when muttering first happened. What I do know is that the bird actually talks to me, and her communication apparently is intended specifically for me. Most of the time no one else even notices. Muttering is more or less a chirp, but very subdued, sort of chirping under her breath. The bird almost gives the impression that she does not want to attract anyone's attention but mine. She could squawk or flap to get everyone's notice, but that isn't what she wants to do.

Muttering always works. When I hear the bird, I invariably get up and give her something. I think it's quite interesting that Jayson mutters only when she sees something on the table that she wants. Fortunately for her, the cage was placed so that she had a "bird's eye" view of the entire table. There are plenty of meals when she doesn't mutter at all, because there is no food on the table that interests her.

For other meals, I actually know in advance that Jayson will mutter, for example, when there are pancakes for breakfast, or spaghetti and meatballs for dinner. These are foods she craves. This aspect of Jayson's behavior probably is a stimulus-response learned behavior. Even so, I think it is important because it shows just how aware Jayson is of her environment and, to the extent that she can, how she tries to control it. I would say this makes for a smart little bird...

Hey, That's Mine!

One of my sisters was visiting a couple of months ago, and whenever she does, she interacts with the bird. She likes Jayson, and always spends time talking to the bird and giving her treats. Jayson, in return, likes my sister, and becomes chirpy and happy when she first comes in. Even though my sister visits infrequently, Jayson readily recognizes her, no matter how much time has gone by since the previous visit.

During her last visit, my sister walked up to the cage and had a "conversation" with Jayson, asking if she wanted a cookie. She was holding a piece of flaky pastry – a cheese Danish, one of Jayson's favorites. My sister held it up to the bird through the bars of the cage, so that Jayson could take it from her fingers. Jayson grabbed the pastry, breaking it with her beak into two big pieces and lots of crumbs. One piece fell on the foam rubber in front of her, while the other one fell behind the edge of the foam at the side of the cage.

A "Hey, that's mine!" moment – Jayson zeroing in on some food that she wants. November 1997.

Thinking the bird couldn't reach the second piece, my sister tried to be nice by picking it up and again offering it to the bird. Jayson's reaction was nothing short of indignant. She snatched the Danish from my sister's fingers, and then dropped it on the foam far from the edge, so that my sister could not reach it. Jayson then proceeded to take all the food she had stashed in that area of her cage (seeds, nuts, and other goodies), and moved all of it to the back of the cage.

My sister was amazed at what the bird was doing, and called me over. I had been watching most of this unfold, and immediately knew what Jayson was up to. The bird was worried that my sister would take her buried food, and she was protecting her cache from a future threat. Jayson appeared to be anticipating something that had not happened, but that *might* happen in the future. This certainly appears to be anticipatory thinking, which requires a higher level of intelligence than simply reacting to events as they occur. I think this is another good example of Jayson's animal intelligence.

Sure, I'll Try That!

I'm quite sure – in fact, I am certain – that none of my dogs would ever spit out food in order to eat something else. It simply is not dog-like. But Jayson does exactly that, showing that she consciously acts upon her food preferences. Through the years there have been dozens of times when I or someone else walked by Jayson's cage holding some food that caught the bird's eye, usually a "cookie," a peanut, or something else she liked. If the bird happened to be eating some lesser food, maybe dog food or seeds, she would come to the front of the cage, chirp a guttural chirp – even if she had a mouthful – and once offered the new tidbit, spit out what she was eating so she could get to the good stuff.

Jayson eating a cornflake after taking a tubby. June 2004.

After eating the cookie, Jayson would go back and finish the food she had spit out. There is no question that Jayson both recognizes specific foods and ranks them by preference. Different foods have different values to the bird, and she makes decisions based on those values. Some foods are highly prized, and others not. Jayson modifies her behavior to get the foods she values most. To me this, too, is the sign of a bright bird. Jayson is without doubt more discriminating in what she eats than my dogs ever were.

First Impressions Matter

Dogs are supposed to be smart animals, and they are. Because I always have had dogs, there is a ready comparison between their intelligence and Jayson's. The bird, I must say, more than holds her own. A good example is the way Jayson deals with people. She consistently is much more selective than my dogs ever have been.

My "watchdogs" would bark at people unpredictably. They always barked at strangers, but many times they even barked at people they knew – people they had no reason at all to bark at. My kids' dogs are the same way. But Jayson never has had this problem. In fact, she seems to take a cue from me as to how to respond to people. The bird always welcomes anyone she knows with a chirpy greeting – that is, if she likes the person – and with a shy retreat to the back of her cage if she doesn't. Unlike the dogs, Jayson never squawks (the equivalent of barking) at anyone she knows.

When it comes to strangers, Jayson initially "studies" them on her own. Then she watches how I react. She always is very quiet, but if I bring a stranger over to her cage, she usually will become friendlier, trusting my judgment, at least most of the time. Sometimes the bird disagrees with me. For reasons only she can know, the bird simply doesn't warm up to some people. Jayson's ability to distinguish people and in some sense to "read" them, I think, requires a high level of intelligence. My dogs sometimes were able to do this, but Jayson does it all the time.

Watchbird

Jayson and our dog Abigail, another German shorthair, developed a cooperative "watch animal" strategy. Abigail was the watchdog, and Jayson the "watchbird." They worked together as a team to warn me of possible threats in the yard, strange people or strange animals. There is no doubt that the bird had better eyesight than the dog, and she also had the advantage of being up high, which gave her a great view. She saw things the dog never would see, like hawks overhead, crows in the trees, other dogs or other animals at a distance, and, more importantly, people.

If Jayson saw something out of place, she squawked in proportion to the danger. A large animal close to the house provoked a much louder reaction than crows far away in the trees. As soon as Jayson squawked, Abigail went to work as her partner, running up to the glass doors barking and looking around intently. Most of the time, Abigail saw the same threat Jayson did, and reacted accordingly. But sometimes she missed it, for example, a hawk circling overhead. But even if she couldn't see the threat, Abigail still barked because she was working with Jayson, who never was wrong.

Jayson's "watchdog" partner, Abigail, the German shorthair.

Jayson's cage was at the back of our house, and consequently the bird had no view to one side or to the front. But the dog did. Because Abigail freely roamed around the house, she could see threats in places Jayson could not. If Abigail barked because she saw some threat, the bird would not automatically respond to the dog the way the dog responded to the bird. Jayson was much more measured in her response. Jayson would crouch low in her cage, looking furtively to see what it was that Abigail saw. If Jayson saw the threat, she would immediately squawk loudly, fulfilling her role as a watchbird. But if she didn't see the intruder, she just kept on looking. Maybe the bird was a tad smarter than the dog?

Jayson, a bird, and Abigail, a bird dog, cooperatively worked together in this way for many years. It was quite amusing to watch them. I think of the way they played off each other as yet another example of Jayson's intelligence. Her performance as a watchbird was at least as good as the dog's. Because the dog is considered a "smart" animal, I think it's fair to say that Jayson must be smart, too.

Christmas Shopping

Cats are naturally very curious animals. Dogs seem to be less curious. The cats I have known enjoy investigating their environment, looking here and there, playing with things they come upon, and generally figuring out what's around them. Dogs seem to pay attention only to certain things, like where the most comfortable sleeping spot is, or what there is to eat. They don't spend much time snooping around the way cats do. Jayson is definitely more like a cat – in fact, if anything, a super cat. She doesn't miss a trick when it comes to knowing what is going on around her.

Because cats and dogs are domesticated, they do not suffer the pressures that wild animals do. In her natural habitat, Jayson could be easy prey for a hawk, or an owl, or a cat, or countless other predators. In order to survive, wild birds must constantly be vigilant. Of course, this trait is innate, something genetically encoded in the bird as part of its survival instinct. The way this trait shows in a captive bird like Jayson is that she notices *everything*. She hears every noise, and she sees every movement, whether it is a person, or an animal, or something else. I know this because I have watched her keep track of what's going on for twenty years.

The holidays are always interesting at my house, among other things because Jayson is so observant. The first time I came home from shopping, the bird went crazy – squawking, flapping all around her cage, crouching, and looking frantically all over the place. I couldn't figure out what the problem was. All I did was walk in the room and place some bags on the kitchen table, which I had done countless times before. Jayson's distress was persistent. I knew something in the environment had set her off, but had no idea what. Figuring it had to be something outside, I looked around, but there was nothing I could spot. Finally, I put my purchases away, the bird eventually quieted down, and we both got back to our usual routines.

After dinner that night, I set about wrapping Christmas gifts. I placed several on the kitchen table, with no reaction at all from the bird. But when I brought out the roles of wrapping paper, Jayson went crazy all over again. It was the roles of wrapping paper sticking half way out of one of the bags that caused her distress that afternoon. Taking the roles out of the room put her at ease – bringing them back caused her to be frantic again. I can only guess it was the shape of the rolls that bothered the bird – long and thin, like a snake. Jayson has reacted this way every time she sees a role of wrapping paper. For the longest time I could not wrap a gift in any place where the bird could see me. The snake idea applies to other things, too.

My husband occasionally putters around with woodworking and couldn't walk by the bird's cage carrying certain types of wood without spooking Jayson. Flat rectangular pieces, like plywood, evoke no response at all. But something like a two-by-four, which is long and skinny, upset the bird tremendously. So did wiffle ball bats, or brooms, or anything long and skinny that Jayson might see as a snake.

Jayson's reaction was especially bad the first time she saw the vacuum cleaner hose. The vac system was built-in, and had a long hose. Jayson just went crazy. To her credit, though, she now has gotten used to the vacuum cleaner hose and doesn't become spooked any more. The bird has adapted to the "hose snake" because she learned that it poses no threat, and to the other "snakes," too. Jayson has learned to distinguish real from imagined threats. Of course, she still reacts to a long, skinny thing that she never before has seen as if it were a snake. The "snake" theory is the only explanation that makes any sense to me, and I think probably it is correct.

So, as far as Jayson's intelligence goes, I am convinced that she is far from a "birdbrain." When it comes to animal intelligence, Jayson really does seem to be on a level with other animals that are considered "smart," like dogs and cats. She is certainly resourceful and clever in creating or learning behaviors that benefit her. She also has adapted very nicely to her environment, and seems to make the best of it. Jayson appears to be quite happy and content. I am convinced Jayson has a very high level of intelligence and adaptability, traits which I believe helped her do as well as she has for twenty years now.

12

Making Pillows?

"It plucked an acorn, grasped it between its strong feet, and hammered the shell open with its sturdy beak."

— Ranger Rick

You wouldn't think that woodpeckers and blue jays have a lot in common, but in some ways Jayson does. I remember one afternoon spending quite a while watching in absolute fascination a large, pileated woodpecker working on a pine tree in the yard. The bird was huge, probably a foot and a half long, with a very large, sharp beak. I had seen many smaller black and white woodpeckers, but never a large one. This bird clung to the side of the pine tree and pecked so hard that I could see chunks of wood flying off. After a few pecks, the bird inspected its work, apparently looking for bugs in and around the hole it had made.

The pileated woodpecker was very effective with its "power pecking," and so was Jayson...

Hard Hat Area!

I always chuckle to myself when I think of Jayson's cage as a hard hat area. I have a silly picture in my head of this tiny blue jay wearing a tiny hard hat as she power pecks her cage. I guess wild jays must peck in a way similar to woodpeckers to get bugs and crack nuts, like acorns, and to bury seeds. That might account for some of Jayson's behavior. I suppose another possibility is that the bird just has fun power pecking. My husband thought that was the answer and placed wooden blocks in Jayson's cage thinking she would enjoy power pecking those as well. But she ignored them. I believe the bird's pecking has to do with stashing food, and she thought of the wooden blocks differently than the floor of her cage. The blocks were like twigs outside, but the cage floor was for her the "ground," a place where she could bury food.

The other thing Jayson consistently did was excavate holes in her foam. Her beak had a very pointy tip, and its edges were quite sharp. She easily was able to dig holes in the foam by pecking it with her beak, grabbing a piece and twisting, and then tearing it off. She did this mostly around the edges of the cage, not so much in the more open middle areas. Jayson used the holes to stash food for a rainy day – seeds, nuts, cereal, and any other goodies she liked. Not only did Jayson bury food in the foam, she also stashed food under it by going to the edge, prying it up, and depositing her treasures. The bird constantly was busy, manipulating the seeds and other food in her cage. She spent hours at it, and to this day still does.

As Jayson's "cleaning lady," it's my job to pick up after the bird, and to prevent some seeds from sprouting, especially ones near her water dish. This was, and still is, a lot of work. Every day Jayson's foam is replaced with clean foam, and the old foam is washed. Jayson is so prolific at stashing food that every few days my husband has to take her out of the cage so I can vacuum it. The bird always has a remarkable amount of food cached, probably enough to last quite a long time, I would guess a week or more. On the days when she's out of the cage, we bathe her in the "sink tubby" – that is, the kitchen sink. If necessary, we clean and medicate her feet. This job primarily falls to Richard – he does the tubby – and I act as his assistant, medicating her feet if needed.

Got Foam?

During the past twenty years, Jayson, the two-ounce blue jay, has gone through hundreds of feet of foam rubber. The foam rubber has worked extremely well in preserving the bird's feet, and using it was a wise choice. The problem with foam rubber is finding it in large pieces. Many stores sell small squares, about a foot on a side (when Jayson arrived we had some leftover pieces from one of the kids' school projects – serendipity again…). But these are too small to cover completely the shelves in Jayson's cage. A continuous piece is best, although two large pieces also work well.

I had no luck at all finding large pieces of foam rubber on my own. Naturally, I was looking in the wrong places. When I mentioned this dilemma to my mother-in-law, she had a suggestion that worked – check at a fabric store (my mother-in-law sews). It was a good tip, because many fabric stores sell foam rubber by the yard. It's used in pillows and other squishy things. I never would have thought that finding a store selling foam rubber would make my day, but it did. Through the years, the sales staff at more than one fabric store have come to know me as a regular customer.

My first visit to the fabric store was quite interesting. After rummaging around for a while, I found the foam rubber off in a corner at the back of the store. It was in long rolls, three feet wide, which was perfect for the bird's cage. I was told that the foam was cut to size like any other bolt of fabric, and that you paid by the yard. All I had to do was go up to the salesperson at the cutting desk and tell her how much I needed. On that first trip I wanted twelve feet, enough to make several shelf covers for Jayson's cage. This way, I always would have a clean piece of foam available.

The response I got was a quizzical look, and a question to the effect "Are you making a lot of pillows?" There happened to be several people in line behind me, who all seemed curious about what I was making. I assume it was because I was buying a lot of foam rubber, at least by usual sewing standards (I don't sew...). One person in line actually asked if I were making a couch...

My reply was "No. You won't believe what I'm buying this for – it's for a blue jay." Whenever and wherever Jayson comes up in conversation, the initial reaction always is the same – confusion, followed by amazement and inquisitiveness as people begin to understand. That day in the fabric store was no different. The question always is "What do you mean, a blue jay?" And this situation has gotten worse with time, because the bird has been around all that much longer.

Whenever I tell someone that a blue jay has lived with my family and me for all these years, twenty at this point, most people just don't get it. It actually takes a while for the idea to sink in. In thinking about it, this reaction isn't all that surprising. Having Jayson around is second nature to me, but it certainly isn't for someone who knows nothing about the bird. Most people have trouble imagining a wild bird living in a house, with people, especially for so long a time. In fact, most people find it quite unbelievable.

The fabric store customers and staff reacted that way. But once they understood exactly what I was talking about, they were fascinated by Jayson's story. Everyone was very curious about how she came into my life and what her situation was – after all, it is quite unusual. They were full of questions, and genuinely interested in how the bird was doing. One question that always comes up is "Do you have a picture?" On my first trip I didn't, but I learned my lesson and now carry Jayson's photo in my wallet, right along with my grandchildren's photographs, of course… What should have been a ten-minute stop at the store ended up taking more than an hour. And whenever I returned, people in the store who knew about Jayson invariably asked after her.

Jayson sitting on the foam on her corner shelf checking out what's on the kitchen table. April 1990.

I soon learned to avoid fabric stores that knew about the bird if I happened to be a hurry, and in other situations not to bring up the bird in conversation unless I was prepared to stick around and explain. Over the years I have spent countless hours telling Jayson's tale to complete strangers in places like the fabric store or pet shops or at parties or other gatherings. In fact, noticing how interested people are in Jayson's story is one of the reasons I decided to write it down. The result is this book, so that you too will know Jayson's story.

Baubles, Bangles, and Beads

Jayson wasn't hard only on her cage and on her foam. She was pretty tough on her toys, too. The bird always has been attracted to shiny objects and to things that make noise. Realizing this, I made an effort to give her interesting bird toys. There are many excellent bird toys on the market, and every pet store has a good selection of them. As it happens, Jayson likes them all – she really gets into toys.

I always had several brand new toys around the house to replace ones that had broken or were old hat for the bird. Every Christmas Jayson received many new toys as gifts, not only from us and the kids, but also from her "grandma" and "auntie." In fact, she even has her own Christmas stocking with her name on it. Every year Jayson's cage is decorated for Christmas – we hang Christmas ornaments and Jayson's stocking from it. The bird does seem to get excited seeing the colorful, shiny new things around the cage. Even the Christmas tree has ornaments with our pet's names – Spock, Annabelle, Baron, Abigail, and, of course, Jayson. In fact, because she has been around so long, Jayson is the only one of our pets that has more than one ornament.

Jayson's corner cage decorated for Christmas. The bird is in front of a nest in the upper left corner. December 1991.

Most of the time, toys had to be replaced because Jayson power pecked them so hard they eventually broke. She could have used a birdie "hard hat" when she played with many of her toys. Whenever Jayson wasn't managing her food supply, she played with her toys, usually a couple of hours every day. She loved ringing bells and making noise with her rattle toys. The bird also liked baby toys, especially the plastic keys infants play with. What she liked most, for some reason, was power pecking them, too. Whenever a new toy was introduced to the cage, Jayson's initial reaction was

Jayson on her small shelf ringing her bell.

to cautiously study the gizmo until she felt comfortable enough to go over and check it out. She then would peck it for a while before actually playing with it. Sometimes this acclimation process took days, but eventually Jayson would get used to the new toy and adopt it as hers.

Jayson also developed a taste for expensive jewelry, especially diamonds. While she likes all sorts of shiny things, diamonds in particular really get her attention. Anyone who puts a hand in Jayson's cage wearing a diamond is likely to have the bird hop over to study the ring. Jayson studies jewelry using her standard inspection technique, lowering her head to get a good view, and moving it from side to side to see the diamond with each eye. It was funny to watch, reminiscent of a jeweler using a loupe. Then she would try to pick up the diamond by gently grabbing it with her beak. Fortunately, through the years, no one had a loose ring setting – I never received a complaint that Jayson swallowed someone's diamond. If she did swallow one, I am sure she would have stored it in her crop, the same way she stored small pebbles.

Jayson's taste in jewelry is not limited only to gemstones. She also likes bracelets, necklaces, and earrings, especially ones with beads or dangling charms. Gold or silver doesn't matter. She wants to play with anything shiny, that's the test. My teenage daughter often played with and entertained the bird by wearing different bracelets and rings and putting her hand in the cage. Jayson very quickly learned that this was a fun game. Whenever my

174

daughter approached the cage, Jayson would hop to the door in anticipation. She pecked and grabbed at any part of the jewelry that caught her eye and tried to pull it off to make it her own. Of course, Jayson never succeeded, but she thoroughly enjoyed trying. This behavior was so ingrained that during a visit to the wildlife clinic, Jayson tried to make off with the technician's diamond ring...

The closest Jayson ever came to having her own "bead" collection was her pebble dish. Her doctor suggested early on that we might want to give the bird a container of small pebbles. He explained that many birds store pebbles in their crop, and that it might benefit Jayson to have some available. For many years, in addition to her seed dish, Jayson also had her pebble dish. I think the bird may have stored pebbles, but I can't be sure. She would pick up a pebble or two and apparently swallow them. But I never could tell if she actually stored them in her crop. She easily could have spit them out when I wasn't looking, and it's hard to keep track of tiny pebbles. I can only assume she stored them the way her veterinarian suggested she would. As Jayson grew older, she eventually began to pay less and less attention to the pebbles. When it became clear that she no longer had any interest in them, I stopped putting the pebble dish in the cage on a regular basis. Every so often I would reintroduce it, but the bird simply had no interest in it, and eventually I stopped altogether.

Where's the Sandpaper?

Over the past twenty years Jayson has lived in four custom-designed and built houses. She lived in house #1 for only two months, thank goodness. This was the chicken wire cage that became her traveling cage (because it was the only one that fit in the back seat of the car). Jayson lived in house #2 for a little more than a year, from October 1984 to late December 1985. House #2 was rectangular in shape, three feet tall, three feet

House #2 in the sunroom (no corner shelf yet). Jayson is on the upper left perch. September 1984.

wide, and two feet deep. When the bird was relocated from the atrium to the kitchen in our new home, late in 1985, Jayson moved into house #3. She occupied this cage, which we called her "corner cage," for about twelve years, until 1998. House #3 was three feet high, about three feet wide, but

House #3, the corner cage in the kitchen. Jayson is crouching on the right main shelf. The atrium is on the left, and the sliding glass door on the right. December 1990.

triangular in shape about a foot and a half deep on left side and about five inches deep on the right.

Jayson's second and third cages shared many common features. They were built with quarter-inch wooden dowels spaced approximately an inch apart. They each had two main shelves on the left and right sides separated by about fifteen inches, and a clean-out tray at the bottom. They also had upper corner shelves to give the bird a place to sleep. And, initially, they had two perches at the top of the cage running from front to back. Both of these cages were donated to the wildlife clinic when Jayson could no longer use them. I have been told that they were put to very good use. Knowing how my husband builds things, I suspect they still are...

Jayson's fourth house, the one she lives in now at age twenty, was designed and built to accommodate her as she aged. The cage was designed in part in anticipation of our moving to Cape Cod, which we did in 1999. We wanted to give the bird a new place to live that would be as pleasant and functional as possible. This cage takes into account how Jayson spends her time now that she is quite old. She no longer can perch, and does not fly anymore, although I believe she could fly if she wanted to.

Like an older person who doesn't want "to do the stairs anymore," Jayson now lives on only one floor, the bottom of her cage, which is, of course, completely covered with foam rubber. She doesn't have a built-in tubby and water dish. In fact, these were removed from her previous cage after she had a seizure, and I saw her fall into the tub. I had not thought of this possibility and the danger it posed to the bird. But as soon as I saw

House #4, the "Greek revival" design. In front of the slider on Cape Cod. Jayson is sitting behind her cuttlebone on the left. July 2004.

this happen, the tub had to go. Now Jayson's water dish is a plastic container that sits on top of the foam, and it does double duty as her tubby, too. She has developed a very effective technique for

179

bathing by splashing herself with water from the dish using her beak. She actually gets quite wet, and usually takes several tubbies each week.

Like the two before it, this cage – house #4 – is about three feet wide and two feet deep, but only about two feet high, with a Greek revival architecture. I asked my husband to space the bars much closer together, so we would not need the unsightly Plexiglas panels installed in house #3 to keep the bird from getting caught between the bars during a seizure. The spacing had to be considerably smaller, and Richard explained to me that quarter-inch dowels would be too big relative to the narrow spacing we needed. The cage would look very odd, sort of like a solid wood panel with narrow grooves cut in it. That would never do, because we wanted the bird to have a good view, and it was also important that we could see her.

After trying different size dowels and spacings, Richard settled on using one-eighth inch dowels spaced one-half inch apart. Because these dowels were flimsier than the big ones, they had to be reinforced with horizontal braces about five inches from the bottom of the cage. This was necessary to make the dowels more rigid near the floor where Jayson spends most of her time. The design also included one upper corner shelf for sleeping, which the bird occasionally used.

When finally we knew what the new cage would look like, the day came when my husband and I set out to buy the materials to build it. We went to a large local general merchandise store that we knew carried everything we needed (after all, we had previously purchased quite a few dowels...). Richard needed around two hundred this time. I was standing next to him as he was bent over the dowel storage bin pulling them out by the handful, counting as he did. He was complaining under his breath that maybe there weren't two hundred in the bin (there were...). While he was doing this, a young woman walked up to him, tapped him on the shoulder asking "Excuse me, sir. My husband sent me in for some sandpaper. Can you tell me where it is?" While I thought this was pretty funny, I don't think my husband did. What I do know is that Richard was happy to be helping Jayson, that was the important thing... and, yes, he told her where the sandpaper was.

- - - - - - - - - -

13

If You're Fond of Sand Dunes...

— *Lyrics from "Old Cape Cod"*

*"Originally a bird of the wild woods, the blue jay
has adapted itself to settlements of man."*
— *Song and Garden Birds of North America*

My husband and I always have been fond of sand dunes, so much so that from when we were first married, we hoped someday to live by the shore. For some reason being near water has a calming effect. In a sense, life is simpler and consequently better. Things that are important in the hubbub of daily living become less important by the shore. When all of our kids finally were on their own, Richard and I decided to move to Cape Cod. I should say, to be more precise, that Richard and I,

and Jayson, and Abigail – we were all on our way to
the Cape!

Dream House

We purchased a lot on a small pond and
designed a small house that reflected our lifestyle.
We always have enjoyed open spaces in a house,
and lots of natural light. The final design centered
on an open family room and kitchen with high
ceilings. Jayson's cage, always having been in the
kitchen, was planned into the design, too. We
wanted to locate the bird between the family room
and kitchen, on the rear outside wall in front of one
panel of a large glass door. This put the bird as
close as possible to people, no matter where they
were, either in the kitchen or in the family room.

In her previous cage, Jayson always had a
good view of the outdoors, and she enjoyed seeing
what was going on outside. Being in front of a
glass door in the new house would give the bird a
panoramic view of the pond, which we knew she
would enjoy. Because Jayson insisted on her
privacy, we decided to hang the cage so that the
bottom third or so was below the edge of the glass,
which placed her corner shelf a few inches above
the edge. When Jayson decided to go to sleep on

the corner shelf, she would not be exposed to the outdoors.

The process of moving to the Cape involved our renting a house for the better part of a year while our new home was being built. Jayson consequently had to get used to a new cage, and to two new houses. I thought this would stress the bird excessively if these disruptions in her life were too close together. Minimizing stress to the bird had become very important, both because of her age and her epilepsy. We couldn't control the builder's schedule, but we could control when Jayson's new cage was built. To minimize stressing the bird, we decided to build Jayson's new cage and move the bird into it several months before relocating to the Cape. This schedule was rather inconvenient for us, because it meant changing the way the cage was hung. But, most importantly, it was better for the bird.

My husband and I sat down one evening and came up with a detailed design for Jayson's house #4 that took into account all of our experiences with the bird over the previous fourteen years. The layout reflected where Jayson spent most of her time, on the bottom floor, and it also took into account her epilepsy by making it impossible for her to fall or to get caught between the bars. The built-in tubby and water dish were combined into a single water dish that sat on the foam rubber instead of in it. Of course, the entire cage bottom and the corner shelf were covered with foam rubber. Another innovation used in the previous cages was also included – wooden blocks to mount her food and seed dishes. These "dishes" actually are plastic container covers attached to the blocks with Velcro. By raising the dishes off the floor, Jayson couldn't step in them, and she didn't have to bend as much to get at her food. These small improvements reduced the stress on the bird's legs and feet.

Jayson's food dishes on wooden blocks (top center & right).

From my point of view, the most important, and best, improvement in the new cage was a very large door that had a latch for closure, instead of ribbons. The day I found Jayson on the kitchen floor many years before, I thought she had opened the cage door by fidgeting with the ribbon that tied it closed. I was wrong, but ever since that day I always worried about the possibility. Using a mechanical latch was much, much better. It was safer for the bird, and more convenient for me. The only reason Richard had not installed a latch on Jayson's previous cage was that there was no door frame to attach it to. In this new cage, the door intentionally was oversized, so that I could easily reach any part of the cage for cleaning and feeding, and it had a frame for the latch.

Through the years we learned that Jayson's power pecking could be very tough on a soft wood like white pine, the type of wood used to build her other cages. The bird regularly power pecked the perimeter of her cage as she stashed food. Sometimes I would see her peck at the wood, tear off a sliver or small piece, and then spit it out. After several years of doing this, Jayson "the woodpecker" had more than made her mark. Richard avoided this problem in the new cage by using rock maple for the bottom and top frames and southern yellow pine for the vertical frame. The new cage turned out to be everything the bird needed, and everything that I wanted. Jayson now has lived in it for more than five years, and she is quite happy there. Many people seeing Jayson's cage for the first time are quite impressed, and several have suggested that Richard go into the business. My husband, well, he just laughs...

Whenever there is anything new in Jayson's environment, the bird has to adjust to it, and the new cage probably was one of her bigger adjustments. Her two previous cages were quite similar, intentionally so, the only major difference being their shapes. Moving between those cages was no big deal. But I wasn't sure how Jayson would react to a totally new house.

It took the bird a couple of days to get used to the new layout, where her corner shelf was, and generally to acclimate to her new digs. What I mean is that during this time Jayson did not settle into her normal routine. After a couple of days, I saw that she was feeling comfortable in the new house, and keeping herself busy by talking to her friends outside, interacting with us, taking her tubbies, and playing with and burying her seeds. I think she liked the extra floor space the new cage provided. She could bounce around burying and digging up seeds over a much larger area, and I know that appealed to the bird. Jayson successfully had completed step one of moving to the Cape –

getting used to the new cage. Her next challenge would be the move itself.

Whoosh!

After months of packing and tossing out fourteen years of accumulated junk – there was a lot of it, especially with five kids – moving day finally arrived. It was May 1, 1999. As we had done in our previous move, some fourteen years before, everything was arranged so as to minimize disturbing the bird. Dozens and dozens of boxes were neatly stacked in the garages and hallways, or anywhere else we could find that was out of Jayson's view. The kitchen and atrium were empty – no furniture, no boxes, in short, nothing at all to be moved from those rooms, so as not to frazzle the bird. It took some planning to organize all of this, and when the day came, my husband and I were anxious to get the move done. My plan for Jayson was to ride with my daughter-in-law, who was making the trek with us specifically to transport the bird. While Jayson's new cage was still too big to fit in the back seat of a car, it fit nicely in the rear of an SUV, which is what my daughter-in-law drove.

Before moving Jayson, my entire house was emptied, my husband and I swept the floors one last time, checked all the nooks and crannies, and said "goodbye" to the old place one last time (I think moving always is bittersweet...). The two of us carried Jayson's cage to the waiting SUV, with the back seat folded so we could slide the cage right up against the back of the front bucket seats. I brought with me a bag of bird goodies – all I had to do to feed Jayson was reach around the side of my seat. Jayson enjoys being fed by hand, as long as she knows and likes the person doing the feeding. The bird took all of this in stride, I think mostly because she was still in her own cage. Staying in her own "house," I am sure, provided an important comfort level for the bird.

But my feelings about the trip were quite different than Jayson's. In spite of my husband's best efforts to convince me of what he called "reason," I just could not get past my anxiety about the bird. She had never before been on a really long trip, and she had never been on a highway. We lived in the woods, and Jayson liked living in the woods. Even Jayson's visits to the wildlife clinic primarily were along country roads. As it turned out, I was right, and my apprehension about the ride well-founded.

Everything went swimmingly, that is, until we got to the highway – Jayson completely freaked out when the first eighteen-wheeler whooshed by us at high speed. Until that happened, Jayson actually had been pretty calm and happy. She would come over for a snack, and I would feed her – there was no obvious stress from the cars around us. It was the big trucks making a lot of noise as they drove by that rattled the bird. Whenever a truck passed us, and there were many, Jayson became very agitated, squawking, flapping, looking frantically from side to side, and jumping around. This situation was intolerable. I told my daughter-in-law to get off at the next exit, so that I could think about what to do. In the meantime, everyone else was well ahead of us on the way to the Cape.

As it turns out, the solution to the problem harked back to when we first got Jayson, many years before when her doctor told us to cover the cage at night. Fortunately, there was a blanket in the car, and all I had to do to calm the bird was drape it over the cage so that Jayson could see only out the front. With the blanket covering the cage and a supply of fresh doughnuts (yes, we made that important stop…), Jayson was fine when we got back on the highway, even as the eighteen-wheelers whooshed by. I attributed her changed behavior to the blanket, but, who knows, maybe, as my daughter-in-law joked, it was the doughnuts…

By the time we arrived at our small rental house on the Cape, Jayson's new digs, everything was pretty much out of the trucks and waiting to be unpacked and set up. Of course, I didn't want to keep Jayson in the car any longer than necessary. So the first thing I did was find a place for her inside, but there wasn't enough time to hang the cage that day. For the time being, Jayson ended up on top of the refrigerator, blocking two cabinets that I really could have used. But it was the only available high place, and, of course, Abigail, the bird dog, was with us, too. Jayson was happy enough in this spot that she ended up staying there for almost a week.

But soon enough Jayson's cage was properly hung from the ceiling, in a corner of the kitchen that gave her a view out of two windows, and a true "bird's eye" view of the table. For Jayson, the outdoor scenery in this little house was only so-so, nothing at all like the beautiful woods she had left. But it was a necessary stepping-stone to what turned out to be an even better location on the pond. In spite of this minor shortcoming, the small rental house turned out to be a very nice place to live for everyone – my husband and I, Jayson, and Abigail. After living there for nearly a year, I must admit there was a certain melancholy when we left.

The Blue Heron

The time finally came when a certificate of occupancy issued for our new home. My husband and I visited the new house probably every other day while it was being built, especially when it was nearly finished. Even though there were the usual problems involved in building a house, we were very pleased with the result. The only family member that never visited was Jayson. Abigail visited the new house several times, sniffing around, getting confused by the unfamiliar floor plan, but instinctively knowing that something was up. I looked forward to the day when we would be in our own home on the pond and settled.

Because this time we were moving only a short distance, about ten miles, none of the problems encountered in moving to the Cape came up. We were able to plan leaving the rental house and moving into the new one with about a week of overlap. It was only after everything actually was in the new house that we carefully transported Jayson in her cage. Her spot was ready, and all we had to do to give her a view of the pond was hang the cage from four chains already attached to the ceiling. This took only a few minutes, and Jayson was in her new home. I breathed a sigh of relief –

now, finally, our relocation to Cape Cod was complete!

I was pleasantly surprised at how quickly Jayson adapted. I suppose the main reason she did so well was that she was not displaced from her cage, and there were no new people or animals around, except for the ones outside. The bird took to her new home very quickly, especially to the pond and the many birds she saw and heard. Jayson really seems to enjoy the view and communicating with her new friends. I think the sunlight glinting off the water also was a major source of fascination for the bird – shiny things always get her attention...

Jayson's pond on Cape Cod.

I am quite sure that the variety of birds she sees interests her a great deal, too. Because Cape Cod is on the Atlantic Flyway, there is a remarkable diversity of birds that constantly changes throughout the year. Many species stop over briefly during their northward or southward migration, and many of these birds rarely, if ever, are seen inland. During one month in mid spring my neighbor, an avid bird watcher, identified fifty-three species in the back yard alone. In many ways, Cape Cod is a birder's paradise. And, of course, Jayson is the ultimate "birder."

There also is no shortage of other wildlife to keep Jayson's interest, from hawks to snapping turtles. In our side yard, there is a hawk's nest, and we regularly have one or two hawks buzzing the pond. There are skylights above Jayson's cage, so she can see hawks and other birds flying above her, which, as far as I can tell, she does do. Jayson certainly sees them flying across the pond, and perching in trees in the back yard as they routinely do. But Jayson's days of vocalizing extensively seem to have passed. The bird hasn't done her hawk imitation in a long time, although she still reacts to seeing them. When a hawk flies by or Jayson catches sight of one on a tree, the bird instinctively crouches, furtively looks around, and sometimes squawks as loud as she can.

Of course, birds are not the only animals that interest Jayson. We have lived in this house for four years now, which has been long enough for Jayson to see many new animals that she never saw in the woods. Each year for the past three years, foxes have crossed my back yard nearly every day for several weeks in the spring and in the fall. The foxes don't show up in the winter or summer, and I have no idea why. But whenever they run through the yard, Jayson sees them and reacts appropriately – squawking her "jay-jay" alarm squawk, flapping, hopping around her cage, and alerting every bird within half a mile. There also are coyotes that visit occasionally. While the foxes seem to have a pretty regular schedule, the coyotes show up unpredictably at irregular intervals, and not nearly as often as the foxes. After watching Jayson's reactions, I can say for sure that she doesn't like coyotes any more than she likes foxes...

The only animals Jayson doesn't seem to mind at all – she never has shown much of an interest in them – are the squirrels and chipmunks. Squirrels raid my birdfeeders just about every day, especially the ones on the deck, about fifteen feet from Jayson's cage. But I don't think even a squirrel convention would faze the bird. My guess is that a symbiotic relationship has evolved between blue jays and squirrels – they're always in the trees together – and maybe chipmunks, too. Or maybe Jayson just thinks of the 'munks as little squirrels...

There is one animal that's a bit mysterious, at least in terms of Jayson's reaction to it – the snapping turtle. A rather large one walks through the yard every spring, going and coming, and I'm pretty sure Jayson sees it. Of course, I have no idea whether or not it actually is the same turtle each year – snapping turtles do tend to look alike. I suppose it is possible that Jayson never sees the turtle, but I think this is highly unlikely, in fact, pretty much impossible. Jayson never misses a trick. The other thought I have is that the turtle moves too slowly to arouse the bird's interest. Whatever the reason, Jayson never has squawked or otherwise reacted when the snapper walks through the yard.

Jayson naturally tends to pay attention mostly to other birds. So it was no surprise that Jayson seemed to be really impressed the day a great blue heron decided to spend some time on our pond. The heron was magnificent, standing at least three feet tall with beautiful grayish-blue feathers, and a truly spectacular beak. It also had a tuft of feathers on its head, much like a blue jay's (I wonder if Jayson was jealous...). I needed binoculars to see these details. But I'm sure Jayson caught them all with her keen eyesight (although lately I think Jayson's visual acuity is deteriorating). Jayson would squawk nervously whenever the heron was in flight, but was quiet and seemed to watch closely when the large bird was fishing at our end of the pond. Unfortunately the heron doesn't stay very long. For the past three years the big bird has stayed on the pond for a few days in the spring and then leaves just as abruptly as it arrived. I'm sure Jayson is disappointed to see it go.

There are other large birds Jayson regularly sees, too – a pair of mute swans, many seagulls and crows, and a variety of ducks and geese. She hears duck sounds for most of the year, and occasionally does her duck imitation in response. The swans appear to be regular summer residents, but, of course, they don't make any noise. The geese are Canada geese that make their characteristic honking sound, but Jayson does not seem to care and shows no interest in mimicking them. Sometimes geese even walk through the back yard, but, except for an occasional crouch, Jayson just ignores them, too. Even though the geese and swans are large birds, Jayson's reaction to them seems to be pretty much ambivalent.

As I write this, in early August 2004, Jayson has lived on this pond for more than four years. She obviously enjoys being where she is. The variety of sounds she hears, almost all birds, and the animals she sees keep her interested and busy. Until about the past year or so, Jayson has been at the back of her cage all day long, looking outside, talking to her friends, and in between grabbing a snack and playing with her seeds. She still spends most of her time there during the day, but recently she has taken to "following" Richard and me if we are close to the cage. The change is subtle, but I see it. I think it has to do with the bird's aging.

When we decided to move to Cape Cod, I was worried about the move's effect on Jayson. Having been here now for more than five years, I know that it was good for us and great for the bird. I hope that Jayson will live out her days in continued good health enjoying the view of her beautiful pond...

- - - - - - - - - -

14

A Pink Bandage

"It is often hard to ignore a bird that is wounded,
exhausted, or orphaned, but most such birds
are beyond saving."
> — *North American Bird Feeder Handbook*

One of the features that most distinguishes different birds is the beak. Birds' feet seem to be fairly similar, one species to another. And birds' wings tend to be more alike than not. But beaks come in all shapes and sizes, and in some cases colors, too, depending, I would guess, on how the beak is used. The beak is more than the bird's mouth – it's actually a tool that is used for all sorts of things. A bird's beak is very important. Unfortunately, right from the beginning, Jayson's was not the best example of a blue jay beak.

Gussied Up

From the very first day Jayson hopped into our lives, it was apparent from looking at her that something was wrong. Neither my husband nor I could put a finger on it. The bird just didn't look right, which is why she ended up at the wildlife clinic. Had Jayson seemed normal in every way, we simply would have let her go. But the bird's appearance and behavior the day she hopped into the garage raised enough concern that we had to have her checked.

Jayson's beak did not close properly at the tip – it still doesn't. A normal bird's beak closes tightly, with the top and bottom perfectly aligned. Jayson's beak not only is not aligned, but the top and bottom are different lengths, with the top usually being longer. This problem has gotten worse through the years, as have her other bone deformities.

Jayson's feet were also malformed. Her toes were skewed to the side, at first only slightly, but with time this also became worse. The first time we saw the bird, her beak and toe problems were so slight that it took very careful observation to notice them, at least for Richard and me since neither of us was trained in what to look for. When Jayson's doctor first examined her, he immediately saw the problems, and he knew instantly what had caused them.

After a few months of Jayson's special dog food and supplement diet, when it was quite clear that her bone deformities could not be reversed, we were confronted with the problem of managing Jayson's beak and feet. Left unchecked, Jayson's beak might continue to grow to the point where she would be unable to eat. When she was young the beak grew quickly, and in a couple of months' time it would become long enough to need a trim.

For a few years – I don't remember exactly how many – Jayson would periodically visit the wildlife clinic for a beak trim and toenail clipping. It was important to me that the bird receive expert medical care, especially while Richard and I were adjusting to how the bird had to be handled. A bird's talon is like a dog's toenail – it bleeds if cut too short. It was quite a long time before my husband and I undertook trimming her beak and talons, but eventually we did.

As time passed, it became more and more traumatic for Jayson to be brought to the clinic. Her reaction was similar to a child's visiting the pediatrician. It became clear to us, and to Jayson's doctor, that the bird would be much better off if her pedicure and "beakicure" could be done at home. Another consideration was that the bird otherwise appeared to be quite healthy, and the notion that she would live only for a couple of years probably was wrong. The bird wasn't subject to either environmental stress or predation – if Jayson died, it would have to be from natural causes.

What this meant for us is that we needed a long-term plan to deal with the beak and talon issues. Always trekking off to the wildlife clinic would not do. During our many trips to the clinic, we watched very carefully how the bird was handled, and how the trimming was done. Finally, I brought the subject up to her doctor. The veterinarian thought that our doing routine maintenance on the bird was a fine idea, especially because we had done so well in caring for her. He gave us instructions on what to do, and what to look for when we trimmed her beak and talons.

Jayson never has liked being handled, even by me – she obviously is not happy when I pick her up. But I am able to put her at ease by stroking her head and talking to her. The bird relaxes and sits still, at least for a short time. But when my husband picks up the bird, her reaction is quite different. She squawks and power pecks Richard's hands, grabbing his skin, and twisting as hard as she can. He does his best to put Jayson at ease, but the bird knows that when Richard picks her up things happen that she does not like.

It's Richard's job to do the beak and nail trimming. This requires two people, but fortunately my role is basically that of assistant. As any "parents" are likely to be, we always have been overly cautious with Jayson. As tough a critter as she is, the small bird is fragile – her small, delicate bones require very careful handling. So my husband and I developed some innovative techniques. I always was very worried about trimming her talons too short, which could result in bleeding. To deal with this contingency, a styptic pencil always is at hand, just in case. Fortunately, for all the years that we have trimmed Jayson's talons, the pencil never has been used.

Because Jayson's talons grew in very odd shapes, and because she squirmed so much, it was difficult to position the nail clipper so that there was no chance of hurting her. An improvised solution to this problem ended up working quite well – the perfect "surgical" tool turned out to be a standard #2 lead pencil, sharpened. While my husband held the little bird in his left hand, I would use the pencil to hold the talon being trimmed away from her foot. The pencil's tapered end allowed me to hold the talon steady while Richard trimmed it using a small nail clipper in his free hand. Because the pencil was placed between the talon and Jayson's foot, it was impossible to accidentally injure the bird. We became quite proficient as a "surgical team," which also was important. The longer Jayson was out of her cage and being worked on, the more traumatic it was for her. We soon were able to trim both feet in just a couple of minutes, which minimized the stress on the bird.

Trimming Jayson's beak turned out to be problematic, too. For one thing, the bird instinctively would pull away whenever we tried even to touch her beak. She would squawk and peck, so that holding her still was very difficult. It was impossible to hold the bird still enough to get the nail clipper onto the very tip of the beak to trim it. Another very real danger was that, in the process of trimming, we might cut her tongue.

Jayson after a "beakicure." May 2001.

Richard cleverly solved this problem using a loosely woven piece of cloth. He would hold Jayson in his left hand and place the cloth over her head. Because she was squawking, and because her beak was always very pointy when it needed trimming, it was an easy matter to get the ends of

Jayson being held by "Dad" after a "beakicure." The tips of the top and bottom parts of the bird's beak were trimmed to allow the beak to close (look carefully at the end of the beak). January 1991.

the beak through the cloth so that the tips were separated. Only the very tips protruded, some distance apart, so that top and bottom of her beak could be separately trimmed to the right length. An added benefit was that the cloth tended to calm the bird because she couldn't see. And Jayson's tongue was completely protected by the cloth. Using this method, we could quickly trim only the end of the beak without stressing the bird too much and without endangering her. Through all the years that Jayson has lived with us, Richard and I constantly have had to develop novel ways of dealing with Jayson's unique problems – fortunately for her we have been pretty successful.

The Shoebox

Medical procedures, I am convinced, are often more traumatic to the family than to the patient. This certainly has been true when one of my kids was the patient. Waiting is without a doubt the worst part, even when there is every reason to believe things will turn out fine. It's quite a bit worse when the doctor tells you up front that there is a substantial risk, which is exactly what happened one day when we brought Jayson in for what should have been a routine visit.

Jayson's doctor decided during his exam that the bird's feet needed surgery, and that it should be done then and there. One of the bird's talons was growing in a spiral that likely would pierce her skin. No amount of trimming would solve the problem – only a surgical procedure would take care of it. I was surprised and disturbed, because I had been under the impression that trimming alone would keep the talons in check. I was wrong.

We were told that the bird would have to be anesthetized, and that she could not leave for at least a couple of hours. Anesthetizing such a small animal is tricky at best, and there was a significant risk to the bird from the anesthesia. None of this was expected when Richard and I brought Jayson in that day. There had been no warning, and we really weren't prepared to deal with the situation. The doctor recommended that we leave and come back late in the day, but neither my husband nor I could do that. When we asked where we could wait, Jayson's doctor wryly said, more or less, "Well, we don't have a waiting room, if that's what you have in mind. But there is a cafeteria up the hill, and you could go there." Of course, that is where we went, three buildings away with not much more to do than watch the clock and sip coffee.

For some reason, when calamity strikes, time goes by either much too quickly, or, as in this case, much too slowly. It's strange how long a minute can be... These perceptions reflected how my husband and I felt about the situation, and they actually surprised even us. After all, Jayson was a wild bird that had been given a "second chance," a good life for a long time, longer by far than she likely would have survived in the wild, even without her medical problems. If she didn't survive the anesthesia, the bird would not even know it. But, in spite of the logic, Richard and I were quite upset and worried, to the point of calling the wildlife clinic several times from the pay phone in the cafeteria. We waited more than three hours before learning that Jayson was okay, and we could pick her up.

Jayson had arrived at the clinic that day, as she always did, in her traveling cage. But her doctor gave us a new means of transport for the trip home – a shoebox with padding inside. Jayson was still groggy from the ether used to anesthetize her, and she could not be safely transported in her own cage. My little bird was gently placed in the shoebox – it was a rather funny sight – and I held it in my lap all the way home. There was a cover for the box, but I didn't need it, because Jayson was too sedated to move around very much. I comforted her as best I could, and, whether it was that or the anesthesia, she did seem relaxed and at ease on the trip back home.

I think – in fact, I am sure – the reason the doctor released Jayson to us when he did was because we had waited all that time. Looking back, it probably would have been better if we picked up the bird later in the day, when she was fully recovered. Fortunately by the time we got home, Jayson was alert enough to be placed in her regular cage, and within a short time she was back to normal. Over the next couple of days, it also became clear that the foot surgery was the right thing to do, because she was able to stand more easily, and now the wild-growing talon was gone and couldn't cause any more problems.

Dial 911

One of my main concerns after moving to Cape Cod was getting Jayson a "personal physician" on the Cape. Not being an HMO member, the bird could not simply choose a new primary care doctor. I had to find one for her, and doing that for a fifteen-year-old blue jay turned out to be much harder than I thought.

I started with our dog's veterinarian, but neither he nor his colleagues was comfortable taking care of a wild bird with Jayson's medical history. His practice was basically a "dog and cat" practice. After calling around, it became quite clear that there were very few veterinarians on the Cape who would treat a wild bird, especially Jayson because of the nature of her problems. No one would take her as a regular patient, although some vets did say they would treat her on an emergency basis if necessary.

Jayson went without a local veterinarian for nearly a year. Our thinking was that the bird was doing well, was stable, and that if anything came up we would be able to find someone in an emergency. But after fully settling into our new home and thinking further about this state of affairs, it was clear that Jayson should have a local doctor who would take care of her on a routine basis.

The only idea I could come up with was to get in touch with the wildlife clinic back home to see if they had any ideas. It seemed reasonable to me that the staff there might know of other vets capable of dealing with a bird like Jayson. I called, and I was told they "would get back to me." Naturally, I expected this, too, would be a dead end. But, no, somewhat to my surprise, about a week later the administrative assistant at the wildlife clinic called and recommended a vet who practiced at a wildlife rehabilitation center on the Cape. The assistant also volunteered to contact the doctor on the Cape, fill her in about Jayson, and let her know that we would be calling. I was thrilled. Serendipity already had been a major player in Jayson's life, and this connection turned out to be yet another example.

It was only a week or so after I had contacted the wildlife clinic when one day, mid-morning, calamity struck. I heard Jayson flapping around her cage making a noticeably different sound than usual. I went over to the cage and was horrified to see blood stains all over her foam. I screamed for my husband. He came running, opened the cage, and picked up the bird. One of Jayson's toes was bleeding and hanging only by some skin. It was obviously broken, and we didn't know what to do.

Richard wrapped the bird in a towel so we could apply gauze to her toe. This succeeded in slowing the bleeding dramatically. Now the question was what to do. Jayson could not be placed back in her cage – she would have continued to bleed. Richard handed me the bird wrapped in the towel, so that he could make some calls. To my surprise, Jayson actually became rather docile, and as long as I was holding her, she quieted down. Jayson is a very resilient little bird, and she adapts very quickly to her physical problems and limitations, even to such a serious injury to her toe.

My husband called the doctor who had been recommended at the rehab center, but was told that she was in an important all-day meeting and could not be disturbed. It was the annual regional meeting of wildlife experts and veterinarians involved in rehabilitation work. Richard persisted, asking the secretary if she would at least slip the doctor a note explaining the emergency nature of the situation. She said she would try.

In the meantime, my oldest daughter, who was visiting at the time, and my husband dug into the phone book. They called every veterinarian they could, but no one would look at the bird. Finally, my daughter succeeded in contacting one doctor's office that would see Jayson at 3 o'clock that afternoon. It was around 11 o'clock in the morning when all this happened, and I could not put Jayson down until we got her to the doctor – the bleeding might start again. At this point, having no other choice, we reluctantly agreed to the 3 o'clock appointment. I would have to try to hold the bird in her towel until then.

Then, just before noontime, serendipity struck again. The receptionist at the rehab center called to let us know us that the veterinarian there could see Jayson at 12:30 on her lunch break, if we wanted to drive over. I was ecstatic. We had just enough time to get there by 12:30, and we all made the trip – Jayson, Richard and I, and my daughter and our year-and-a-half old grandson. My daughter has a special relationship with Jayson – it was her hair the bird would pull out, and her jewelry Jayson tried to steal. She had to be there "for the bird."

I held Jayson in my lap in the passenger seat while Richard drove my daughter's car because we needed the toddler's car seat. In the back were my daughter and grandson, and Jayson's newest traveling cage, a bright pink plastic laundry basket with a snap-on cover (when we moved to Cape Cod, Jayson's old chicken wire traveling cage finally was retired). But that day, in late spring of the year 2000, Jayson rode in style, in my lap, going and coming. Jayson was happy, wrapped warmly in her towel and having her head stroked as we drove. So even on the way back I didn't bother with the laundry basket.

When we met the veterinarian, the doctor's immediate reaction was complete surprise. About a week before this happened, the administrative assistant at the wildlife clinic had called the vet and explained Jayson's situation, just as she said she

Jayson in her laundry basket during a cage cleaning. July 2003.

would do. But she gave the vet only a general description of the bird's situation. She had not been very specific about Jayson's malformed feet or her other medical problems. The vet naturally assumed Jayson was coming in for a routine visit, not for an emergency.

I forever will be grateful to this doctor for giving up her lunch break on a busy day to see Jayson for what she thought was just a routine check-up. Of course, this visit wasn't even close to routine. The doctor was shocked to see Jayson's toe hanging by a piece of skin and bleeding. She told us there was no choice other than to amputate the digit, and, as we had been told before, explained the risk of anesthesia. At this point in Jayson's life, the risk was compounded by her advanced age (nearly sixteen at the time). But neither we, nor the bird, had any choice.

Jayson was anesthetized and her toe removed. Cauterizing the wound stopped the bleeding. When the bird came out of surgery, she was groggy, as she had been previously after anesthesia. But otherwise she was doing fine – and sported a bright pink bandage on her foot. I never did ask the doctor if there were a choice of colors, but I am quite happy that Jayson's was pink. Even though she is a blue jay, she is, after all, a girl.

I wish we had photographed Jayson's pink bandage, but we didn't. At the time, and pretty much throughout the past twenty years, the thought simply didn't cross my mind. Now looking back, there were countless times when perhaps a picture should have been taken, or a recording made, or maybe some sort of diary kept about the bird. But none of this was done. As a result, the photos I have of the bird are haphazard and usually far apart, most often taken on some occasion, a holiday, a birthday or graduation party, that sort of thing. I went through all the pictures I have of Jayson, and I included in the book the ones that show something interesting about the bird. I hope I have succeeded.

Lest I digress too much, after her surgery Jayson did very well once she was back at home in her own surroundings. The bird obviously felt much better. And she looked so cute in her new pick bandage, hopping around quite spryly on it! A few days later she was brought back to have the bandage removed, and she has not experienced any toe problems since this frightening episode four years ago.

When Jayson went back to the rehab center a few days later to have her pink bandage removed, as you can imagine, the atmosphere was much more relaxed. Richard and I were able to calmly talk at length with her doctor. The vet was very curious about Jayson, her medical problems, and how we had dealt with the bird for what was then nearly sixteen years. We filled her in as best we could, and basically the message to us was "Keep on doing what you're doing." Jayson's new "personal physician" was amazed, both at the bird's age and her condition given her age. There was no reason to change anything.

Then, in a curious twist, Jayson's new vet told us how it happened that the bird's "old" doctor from the wildlife clinic was at the meeting the day her toe was amputated. When it came out in conversation that a blue jay named "Jayson" had been operated on over lunch, Jayson's old doctor explained how he knew the bird. He was totally flabbergasted that she was still alive after sixteen years, and doing so well. Jayson's new vet complimented us on what we had done for the bird. Needless to say, Richard and I were truly pleased to hear such positive remarks. Comments like hers help make the twenty years that we now have invested in Jayson worth it. Then, as we were leaving the rehab center, there was one last surprise – when Jayson's doctor asked if we would be interested in doing rehabilitation on other birds...

– – – – – – – – – –

15

The Junk Drawer

*"They have a violent dislike of predators,
and their raucous screaming makes it easy
to locate a hawk or a roosting owl."*
— *Field Guide of North American Birds*

Everyone has a drawer filled
with things that don't seem to fit anywhere else. I
have one of those drawers – in fact, more than one.
In many ways, trying to organize a book is like
organizing the drawers. Well, if you have managed
to read this far, besides getting my thanks, you have
arrived at the chapter where I write about things that
don't seem to fit anywhere else. This is the junk
drawer in Jayson's story.

Stairway to Heaven

Every one of my five children has at least one pet. All of their pets have been dogs, until, sadly, a couple of years ago, when my youngest son's dog passed away quite unexpectedly. He and his dog Max were best buddies, and Max was a wonderful example of a well-trained, friendly German shepherd. All of us miss Max. According to the other kids, my boy "turned traitor" by replacing Max not with another dog, but instead, of all things, with a cat. My son now lives in an apartment in the city, and a cat is clearly a better pet under the circumstances. It was a sensible choice, and he very much enjoys the cat's company. He often visits us on the Cape, usually without the cat. But two years ago he stayed with us for most of the summer – he's a teacher – and because of the extended stay, Catzilla was here for the entire time, too.

Zilla (or "Zill"), as she fondly is called, had never before seen Jayson. I remember the day Zill arrived as if it were yesterday. She is the typically curious feline, and I don't think two minutes went by before the cat noticed the bird. Zilla was a shelter cat, and apparently had lived outdoors for some time. When the cat saw Jayson, she became transfixed. I have no doubt this was a "died and gone to Heaven" moment for the cat... But, in an interesting contrast, Jayson just ignored Catzilla, I suppose because she never before had seen a cat. Jayson doesn't like big animals, especially furry ones. The smaller the animal, the less important it seems to be to Jayson. It isn't that Jayson didn't see the cat – of course, she did. But she was dismissive of it, no big deal in the bird's mind.

Zilla, not surprisingly, saw things quite differently. Every day for nearly two months Zill tried to get at the bird. Fortunately, she never even got close – we made sure of that... But Jayson always was on Zill's mind. I know this because I watched the cat like a hawk, and Zilla was put in the basement if there was no one home to keep an eye on her and Jayson. Even though it seemed unimaginable that the cat could get at the bird, I wasn't about to take even the slightest chance.

Our house on the pond has a large, open family room and kitchen area with cathedral ceilings. The top of the kitchen cabinets is a shelf, which I use for knick-knacks and plants because of the high ceilings. This shelf is readily accessible from the second floor balcony, especially for an agile cat. Zilla figured this out the first day she was here. She would walk upstairs onto the balcony, hop onto the top of the nearest cabinet, and from there go to the cabinet closest to the bird. This gave

View from the balcony showing the cabinets on the right and Jayson's cage in front of the slider on the left.

the cat a great view of the bird, because she actually was a bit higher than the cage. Unfortunately – for Zill, that is – she couldn't get any closer than about twenty feet, which left only the balcony itself as an approach to the cage.

The edge of the balcony was closer and higher, but not nearly close enough. The only way Zilla could make it to the cage from there was to leap across the kitchen, over the kitchen table, a dis-

Zilla stalking Jayson on the cabinets…

tance of about fifteen feet. Whenever Zill positioned herself on the balcony, or on the cabinets, anyone watching could see the cat doing the mental arithmetic that cats do to make the jump. But she always came up short, and never even attempted the leap…

Over time, as Zill became desperate, she adopted a more frontal strategy. The cat would walk over to the cage, park herself directly beneath it, and every so often jump straight up off the floor, front paws – and claws – extended as fully as possible, hoping somehow to grab onto the cage. But she was a small cat, and the cage was nearly six feet off the floor. Zill simply couldn't jump that high. She actually seemed to enjoy trying, and we certainly found her antics humorous, especially because Jayson, the intended victim, was totally oblivious. Eventually the summer came to an end, and Zilla went back home a very frustrated little cat.

My husband and I rarely are gone more than overnight, but sometimes we would be away for a few days. On these occasions we arranged for bird sitters, always one of the kids because they know the bird and how to care for her. Of course, from their point of view it's not such a bad deal – a few days on Cape Cod without mom and dad around... On one such occasion, my son came to the Cape to bird-sit for a long weekend. He brought Zilla with him, which turned out to be a surprise to me. This took place several months after Zilla's summer vacation with us. Naturally, the cat had not forgotten Jayson, and she did her best to get at the bird by capitalizing on some changes in the house. On this visit, Zilla discovered, to her delight, a tall plant stand I had placed near Jayson's cage. The plant stand has four shelves, each separated by about eighteen inches.

On the second day of our trip, I received a call from my son, letting me know for the first time that he had to bring the cat with him, and, jokingly, that he had to rearrange the furniture. Zilla was absolutely thrilled to discover the plant stand. According to my son, Catzilla finally had found the "stairway to Heaven"... My husband and I enjoyed our long weekend, Jayson did fine, and, as usual, and Zilla went home still frustrated. Whenever Zilla visits, she is single-minded in her pursuit of Jayson, and we are very watchful as a result. Whenever I think about the cat and the bird, I am sure you know what comes to mind – the cartoon, of course – Jayson is Tweety, and Zill is Sylvester.

Zilla's "stairway to heaven," the plant stand that had to be moved. Jayson is sitting at the back of the cage looking out at the pond.

Mesmerized

Occasionally Jayson does something *very* strange. The mammals in our lives, especially domestic pets like cats and dogs, behave in more or less predictable ways. Even their "odd" behaviors aren't really all that unusual. I once read a magazine article about the evolution of birds. It showed a small dinosaur morphing into a bird – a blue jay as a matter of fact. I am guessing that Jayson's odd behavior in this case has to do with the fact that her distant relatives probably were small dinosaurs. Lizards are cold-blooded, and consequently sunlight is very important to them. Without the warmth of the sun lizards can't live. This sensitivity to the sun may account for Jayson's strange behavior, even though she is not cold-blooded.

The first time Richard and I noticed it was in the spring of 1985, one day when we cleaned Jayson's wooden cage. It was a gorgeous, unusually mild, very sunny early spring day. The sky didn't have a cloud in it, and the sunlight was intense. The weather was so nice we thought the bird would enjoy being outdoors while we cleaned her cage on the deck. Jayson was put in her chicken wire traveling cage, which we placed on a patio table on the deck.

At first Jayson seemed uncomfortable. For the bird I think actually being outdoors was quite different from looking out from the inside. It took her a while to settle in. As usual, I could tell when she did by the way she moved and how she behaved. When Jayson is comfortable, her movements are deliberate and fluid. When she is uncomfortable, her movements are erratic. After acclimating to being outside, the bird seemed to enjoy it quite a bit. She was looking around, occasionally answering another jay's call, and as usual playing with her seeds. Richard and I nonchalantly went about the business of taking apart and cleaning her cage. All the while, Jayson was only a few feet away.

Today, nearly twenty years later, I can't recall whether it was Richard or I who first noticed the bird. What I do remember is that we were both completely taken aback by what Jayson was doing – there she was on her corner shelf with her wings spread out as far as possible, absolutely still, with her head tilted so that one eye looked directly at the sun!

Richard and I walked cautiously over to the cage. We were able to walk entirely around the bird, fairly close to the cage, with no reaction from her whatsoever. This was very strange. Normally, doing this would cause Jayson to react by hopping around and either chirping or squawking, but not this day. The bird was completely oblivious to our

Jayson in a sunlight trance. May 1988.

presence. She acted as if she were in a trance, literally. The sun had somehow mesmerized the bird. When we obstructed the sun by casting a shadow over the cage, within several seconds the bird became normal again. If we then allowed her

227

to gaze directly at the sun, she would go back into the trance.

Sunlight trance. May 1988.

Falling into the "sunlight trance" is by far the most bizarre thing that Jayson ever has done. There have been many occasions since that first day when she has gone into her sunlight trance, both outside when her cage was being cleaned, and even in the house when the sunlight strikes her in just the right way. Looking at the bird when she is mesmerized, both my husband and I get the unmistakable impression that Jayson is attempting to "collect" the sunlight. I do believe this goes back to her dinosaur ancestors and their instinctive desire to stay warm. Whenever I imagine Jayson spreading her wings with the bright sun shining in her eye, I can't help but go back to that first day on the deck nearly twenty years ago – it certainly made a lasting impression, and I smile whenever I think of it.

Speaking "People"

Humans strive for proficiency in more than one language. To some degree animals do, too. Dogs and cats have demonstrated "people" vocabularies, that is, they learn to understand "people" as another language by mastering specific words. Smart dogs are known to understand dozens of words, and their vocabularies can be measured. I never have attempted to measure Jayson's vocabulary, but I know she understands the meaning of many words. If I had to come up with the bird's vocabulary list, at a minimum I would include the following: Jayson, Abigail, Baron, Annabelle, peanut, cookie, cracker, seed, drink, bath, and tubby. There is no doubt in my mind that Jayson actually connects these words with what they mean. I suspect there are many other words that she understands as well, but I cannot say for sure. I think she recognizes people's names, like mine or my husband's or the kids'. Knowing

Jayson, I suspect she understands many more words than I would guess, because, after all, she is a smart little bird.

Reflections

Anyone who has lived in a house surrounded by trees, and who pays attention to wildlife, probably has had the sad experience of finding a bird that flew into a window, or, worse yet, actually witnessing it happen. Birds see the reflection of the trees behind them in the window, and fly straight ahead into what they think is a stand of trees. Under the right lighting conditions, a window acts as a mirror to the bird. Jayson, thankfully, could not fly into a window because she always was in her cage. But she certainly could use one as a mirror. And, being the clever bird she is, she did.

One day while I was sitting in the kitchen, I noticed Jayson going into crouch mode. She began squawking loudly. She obviously saw something outside, probably an animal, and I got up to look. I looked all around the backyard, and saw absolutely nothing. I also heard nothing. In fact, it was curiously quiet outside. Jayson rarely, if ever, is wrong. There definitely was something afoot – I just couldn't see what it was.

Jayson's cage was positioned so that she could see only about half of the backyard. When I carefully looked at the bird, what I noticed was that she seemed to be looking intently into a part of the yard that she couldn't actually see, which I thought was very odd. The view was blocked by part of the house, the family room, which protruded from the back of the house along one side of the deck. Where the family room met the deck, more or less perpendicular to Jayson's line of sight, there was a large picture window. As I watched the bird, it became clear that she was not looking into the yard at all.

Jayson was staring at the picture window. I then looked in the direction opposite to Jayson's gaze, and, much to my surprise, there was a very large owl in a tree. It actually was difficult to see, because owls are so well camouflaged. The owl was perched on a branch, sitting very still, not making any noise. Jayson obviously was reacting to the owl's reflection in the picture window. I am sure Jayson saw that owl as clearly as if she looked directly at it. To Jayson, the owl was a real threat, and she reacted accordingly. This particular owl lived in the woods behind the house, and we saw it regularly. Whenever Jayson saw it, either directly or by reflection as she did this day, she would warn all her friends outside, and crouch as low as possible to avoid being the owl's next meal.

Shaggy Dogs

You wouldn't think that hairdo would matter to a bird, but it does to Jayson. At least other animals' hairdos do. Through the years we have had many friends visit with their dogs, which has given me a good opportunity to observe how Jayson reacts to them. Jayson's reaction to different dogs has been quite consistent through the years. There appears to be a clear demarcation between the dogs that Jayson tolerates and the ones she does not – the line has to do with size and hairdo.

Jayson does not mind small dogs, any small dog as far as I can tell. For example, my brother and his fiancée visited a couple of months ago with her dog Joseph, a small Pekinese. It was his first time here, and Joseph fit right in, scampering around the house, and looking up at Jayson's cage when she fluttered. The bird's reaction to Joseph was a complete lack of interest, which was more or less mutual. Joseph paid attention to the bird only when she made noise, and Jayson went about her business as if Joseph were not even here. The little dog could have been invisible to the bird.

Jayson does not mind small dogs – or cats – of any kind. And she doesn't mind big dogs with short fur either. My oldest son's dog is an eighty-five pound jet black lab named Molly. Jayson is just as ambivalent when Molly visits as she is when Joseph is around. The same applies to my younger daughter's German shepherd, Otis, and also to my youngest son's dog Max when he was alive. My older daughter has two medium sized dogs, one of which, Coco, has very short fur, while the other, Nella, has rather long fur, but isn't very big. Jayson doesn't mind having any of these dogs around. But the bird's casual attitude changes dramatically when there are big, furry dogs around – size and fur matter a lot.

It was probably fifteen years ago when one of my sisters and her husband stopped by with their English sheep dog, Misty. Misty was very big, and very furry, and for some reason scared the daylights out of Jayson. As long as Misty was in view – inside or out, it made no difference – Jayson squawked frantically. The bird simply would not calm down, even though Misty showed absolutely no interest in the bird. As soon as Misty was removed from view, Jayson regained her composure. But as soon as Jayson could see Misty, the bird fell apart.

Several years later, some friends stopped by for an afternoon visit and had with them their dog, whose name I can't remember. What I do remember, and what Jayson certainly noticed, is that the dog was quite large with long, white fur, sort of like a Collie's. Jayson went crazy the instant she saw the dog. The only way we could calm the bird was to put the big white dog where Jayson could not see it.

The bird's behavior remains the same to this day. Last year some friends visited and brought with them their two Newfoundlands, Ruby and Mariah. The poor dogs spent the entire day tied in the backyard, because Jayson simply would not stop squawking as long as they were in sight. What also is interesting about this idiosyncratic behavior is that none of these dogs posed the slightest overt threat to the bird. Every one ignored the bird, acting pretty much as if she weren't there. These dogs did not bark, or jump, or even pay much attention to Jayson. Yet Jayson apparently was terrified.

The only minor exception to Jayson's intense dislike of large, furry dogs is perhaps my middle boy's dog, Murray. Murray is a large mongrel – but not too big – a pound dog with very long fur. Murray is very shaggy, and for a long time Jayson reacted to him the same way she would to other large, shaggy dogs. But over time, she has grown accustomed to Murray, more or less. She doesn't squawk up a storm whenever she can see him. Still, even now, she is noticeably skittish when Murray visits. Jayson seems to be more wary and to keep an eye on him when he's in view, even though she doesn't squawk that much.

Try as I might, I cannot figure out exactly what it is about dog stature and fur that sets Jayson off. The correlation is very strong – the bigger the dog, and the furrier, the more intense is Jayson's reaction. Interestingly, the color seems to make no difference. Misty was gray and white; the dog whose name I can't remember was pretty much all white; and Murray's coat is brown-black-tan. There's just something about big, shaggy dogs that Jayson does not like, and she lets everyone know it...

– – – – – – – – – –

16

You're How Old?

"The lives of most common birds are surprisingly short... In general it is the healthiest birds that survive the hazards of the first months of life and that continue the species."
— *North American Bird Feeder Handbook*

There is a strong tendency, almost a compulsion it seems, for people to "humanize" our animal friends. We constantly attribute human traits to animals, even though we know how silly this is. Measuring an animal's life span is an example. Everyone knows that a "dog year" is the equivalent of seven human years. I am pretty sure this is because dogs live about ten years, while human life expectancy is around seventy years, or at least it was when the dog year-to-human year equivalence was invented. Applying the same logic to jays, a "blue jay year" is equivalent to thirty-five human years, because blue jays live about two years in the wild. That makes Jayson seven hundred years old! Wow, she must be one of the oldest blue jays on the planet...

Jayson sitting on her perch when she was young. 1985.

No Gray Feathers

I don't know whether or not birds turn gray the way people do. Dogs certainly do, as do cats. I seem to recall reading somewhere that very old birds actually do turn gray, but I honestly don't know if this true. Even if it were, in Jayson's case it might be very difficult to tell – after all, she does have a lot of gray feathers.

But there is another "color" measure of Jayson's youthfulness. Her doctor pointed it out to us about six years ago during a routine visit. The vet was surprised to see the bird's mouth so pink in a fourteen year old bird. The pigment in a jay's mouth usually darkens noticeably as the bird ages. The vet said that Jayson's mouth looked like one in a much younger bird. By this measure Jayson may have seemed surprisingly youthful. But the truth is, Jayson definitely has shown substantial physical signs of aging through the years.

One such sign is a cataract in Jayson's left eye, which I noticed only recently. Cataracts go along with old age, in a sense just a variation of "gray feathers." Jayson's eye appears cloudy, and when I mention it to other people, they immediately notice it, too. My "diagnosis" is based on everyday experience with people and other animals (my dogs had cataracts), not on any medical training. I haven't been able to confirm this diagnosis with Jayson's personal physician, because the bird has not made an office visit, thankfully, in several years. In fact, the last time she saw her doctor was when the pink bandage was removed four years ago. As Jayson has aged, especially during the last few years, I have been more and more reluctant to take her out unnecessarily because it does stress the bird. Fortunately, ever since her toe was amputated, Jayson has been stable and has not experienced any medical problems requiring a trip to the vet. The few minor issues that have come up I have been able to deal with over the phone.

Those Tired Old Bones

Jayson also shows her age in her bones. Throughout the past twenty years the deformities have gotten progressively worse. Once, years ago, the bird was able to perch quite nicely, but it has been a very long time since that was possible. The effect of this gradual deterioration has been to limit Jayson's mobility, but to the bird's great credit she has adapted even to that, by bouncing around her cage on her deformed feet. In a way, like a three-legged dog, Jayson has fully accommodated this disability, and is quite the happy little bird in spite of it. The bone problems certainly haven't stopped her from doing what she wants to do around her cage, except, of course, perch.

Out of Steam

Like a person growing older, Jayson also shows her age in her energy level. I have noticed that she goes to sleep earlier than she used to, and occasionally even nods off during the day – sort of a birdie "power nap." In years past, Jayson never went to bed before us, and never napped during the day. I always would say goodnight to the bird as I shut the lights, and she would chirp back an acknowledgment, almost like saying "good night to you, too – see you in the morning."

These days, the bird usually is fast asleep when I retire, and she no longer stays up even when there is company, with the lights on and a lot of commotion. Jayson never would have missed a party in her younger days. There were too many interesting things to watch and too many opportunities to get a treat for her to go to bed early! To accommodate Jayson's new bedtime schedule, I now dim the lights early, so she can go to sleep whenever she wants. These days it is rare that Jayson stays up very late at all.

Jayson doesn't fly any more, either. When she was younger, she flew from perch to perch, up and down between the main shelves and the corner shelves, or from corner shelf to corner shelf. The bird spent a fair amount of time doing this because each of the places she visited held some interest for her. It might be a better view of something outside, or on the table, or even in the cage. It might be getting to a food stash to retrieve a tidbit, or going to bury something off in a corner. But, sadly, over time Jayson has flown less and less. The process was quite gradual, over a period of many years. Now Jayson basically does not fly at all. She still has her corner shelf, but she shows no interest in it, and it is very rare that I see her on it. I think it's simply too much work for what is now a very old bird. Even though I know Jayson can do it, fly up to that shelf, or maybe take a spin around the cage, for her it appears not to be worth the effort...

Well, They Wouldn't Hatch, Anyway

There are other physical signs that show Jayson's age. It has been ten years or so since the bird laid an egg. The first time she laid eggs, she produced four of them. For about nine years Jayson continued to lay eggs, but, with time she produced fewer of them at less frequent intervals. When

241

Jayson was young, she laid eggs twice a year, in the spring and in the fall. As she got older that schedule changed, and she produced eggs only in the spring. She also gradually produced fewer and fewer eggs, until finally she would lay only one at a time. Then one year the bird stopped producing altogether, and she never has laid an egg since. Jayson's physiology obviously has changed through the years, so that this once prolific little bird no longer has the ability to produce eggs – yet another sign of her aging.

Jayson's age also shows in her beak and her toenails. They now grow much more slowly than when she was younger. What used to be a fairly regular trimming schedule, initially every couple of months, has gradually spread out and now is only occasional. We have not had to trim the bird's beak more than a couple of times in the past two years – it simply hasn't been necessary. At this point in Jayson's life, with her being twenty years old, the beak grows so slowly that when its tip is a bit too long, she tends to break it by power pecking. This natural process trims the beak, so we don't have to. The fact is, this is much better for the bird, because she definitely doesn't like being given a "beakicure." Nonetheless, I do carefully look the bird over every morning, and if she needs a quick trim, she gets it.

242

Turn That Down, Please

One of the saddest things I have noticed about Jayson's aging is that she no longer is interested in sounds the way she once was. I don't remember exactly when the bird stopped ringing with the telephone, but it was several years ago at least. Some of Jayson's most comical moments were the times she would ring with the phone, wildly bobbing up and down, having a grand old time, usually at my expense with the person on the other end of the line. As much as it created a problem for me during the years I operated my business from the house, I must say I do miss Jayson's ringing and bobbing. I would gladly put up with any inconvenience if she started again, but that will not happen – the bird is too old.

I don't think the reason Jayson stopped ringing has anything much to do with her physical condition. She still makes plenty of noises, and at various times still makes all of the unusual ones she used to make. Even now Jayson gurgles, trills, clicks, whistles, and makes all sorts of other sounds. What has changed is that now she does the more exotic sounds only very rarely. The sounds she makes most these days are her instinctive responses, like the "jay-jay" alarm squawk, or her crow imitation when she sees crows outside. Jayson has given up performing her most interesting sounds, such as making up and singing her own songs, or singing along with music she likes, or doing something crazy like ringing with the phone. I think the bird simply lost interest. Vocalizing is Jayson's behavior that I miss the most. I would do almost anything to have the bird singing, and ringing, and bobbing again…

Goin' to the Couch

Jayson always has been an independent minded little bird. She does what she wants to do without much consideration of what is going on around her, or who might be nearby, unless, of course, there is something in it for her. Naturally, this is quite understandable, and, when I think about it, a lot like the way my kids behave…

As Jayson has gotten older, she has in a sense become less "independent." When she was younger, the bird was in every corner of her cage all day long, constantly flitting from one place to another, seemingly on a whim, until finally she went to sleep. The bird constantly was busy, and, until it was bedtime, never got tired – she had endless energy. For the longest time, the bird just did just what she wanted to do, flitting around and,

Jayson showing her age. 12 June 2004.

for the most part, ignoring us – after all, we were just the "hired help." But within the last year or so, there has been a very noticeable change – now Jayson tends to park herself close to my husband and me, and she isn't as busy as she used to be.

These days, any time we sit at the kitchen table, not only for meals, Jayson comes to the corner of her cage nearest the table, sitting quietly and watching. In years past, the only time she did this was at dinner. Jayson still mutters, by the way, which is a vocalization she has not given up, and which I still enjoy immensely. Now, whenever my husband and I sit on the couch in the family room watching TV – time of day doesn't matter – the bird moves to the opposite corner of her cage, the one closest to the couch. She sits quietly and watches us watch TV, or maybe she watches TV herself – it's hard to tell. But in years past, the bird would do this only if we were watching a show she liked. Now, whenever Richard and I sit on the deck, Jayson goes to the back of the cage, the area that's nearest the deck, even if it is late and the sun has set. In years past, when the sun went down, Jayson spent most of her time towards the front of her cage.

As we move around the house now, especially late in the day when the bird tends to be more subdued, Jayson "follows" us. She always seems to place herself closest to where we are, and she always seems to be paying attention to what we are doing. Anyone not knowing the bird never would notice this. It is subtle, but I see it. I have lived with Jayson long enough to know that she actually is following us. The only exception seems to be during the day if Richard and I are off somewhere. I frequently work in the yard, for example, but I'm in and out of the house. When no

Jayson and I. August 2004.

one is inside, or when no one is close enough to the cage, then Jayson tends to be at the back of the cage where she can look out and see what's going on in the yard and on the pond.

I am sure Jayson's new behavior is connected somehow to her growing older, but I

247

have no idea exactly how. I remember how the bird pined away the first time we moved and hung her cage in the atrium, away from where the people were most of the time. Jayson needed to be close to her "family" then – perhaps this urge has become stronger as she has gotten older. What I can say for sure is that the bird's "following" behavior gradually has developed over the past year or so and now appears to be quite entrenched. Jayson doesn't like being left alone anymore…

As I close this story, in August 2004, thankfully Jayson still is with us. This little blue jay has outlived three dogs and a lizard – now there are just the three of us. She has shown her age quite a bit this past year in many different ways, but the bird appears still to be healthy and happy. Jayson enjoys her days doing all her usual things, but at a slower pace. She still is perky, jumping around her cage, or taking a tubby in her water dish, or mimicking a crow outside.

At this point in her life, I think Jayson actually enjoys the quieter, more peaceful moments too. When our kids visit with our six grandchildren, and with their dogs or with Zilla, Jayson really seems to enjoy their company. But, like us, she also enjoys it when everyone goes home, and things quiet down again. At the end of the day, Jayson

looks out at the sun setting on the pond and quietly
goes to sleep…

- - - - - - - - - -

Digital "white board" photo of Jayson. 1 August 2004.

Epilogue
4 August 2004

"The hazards in a bird's life mean that it will be lucky to live beyond a couple of years."

— North American Bird Feeder Handbook

I always have thought that caging an animal is cruel.   I never have liked zoos, although I suppose the modern ones that allow animals to roam are an improvement.   When Jayson failed her flight physical, the bird was condemned to a fate certain – she would be euthanized, because she could not survive in the wild.   It was a stark choice – die peacefully and calmly at the hands of a human dedicated to preserving and helping wild animals, or inevitably suffer a painful and possibly violent death in the wild.   Jayson had no place to go.   My husband and I also were confronted with a stark choice – leave the little bird, knowing full well what would happen to her, or take her, "rescue" her, knowing that she would live in a cage for the rest of her life.

I don't believe a blue jay knows the difference between two years and twenty years – but, of course, I do. From what we were told twenty years ago, I expected Jayson to live a couple of years in captivity, maybe a few if she were lucky. Richard and I both thought that a couple of years in a large cage, warm and comfortable with good food, no predators, pleasant surroundings, and plenty of company, was a reasonable alternative for the bird. I think the veterinarian saw it that way, too, which is why we were allowed to keep the bird. For twenty years now we have kept Jayson in a cage, for her sake. In looking back, I think we did the right thing. Would I do it again? Yes, without hesitation.

Jayson has had an interesting and healthy life, which is far better than she would have had on her own in the wild. The fact is, a bird's world is a very hostile place. Besides, Jayson probably never knew true freedom – if anything, the world for her likely was a harsh and frightening place, not some idyllic flower-filled garden where the birds tweet all day long. I don't think that being caged even for all these years has been a real loss for Jayson. Of course, I never did – or, for that matter even could –

contemplate the possibility that the frightened little blue jay who hopped into my garage on August 4 of 1984, exactly twenty years ago today, and who was supposed to live "maybe two years," actually would be with me for twenty… And counting…

Jayson

Chapter Headnotes

Ch. 1   *"Blue Jays are among the most intelligent and opportunistic of North American birds..."* North American Birdfeeder Handbook, Robert Burton, National Audubon Society, 1995, p. 197.

Ch. 2   *"Lots of people love 'em. Other people hate 'em. But most people agree that blue jays are bright, beautiful birds."* Ranger Rick Magazine, National Wildlife Federation, Sallie Luther, April 1991, p. 22.

Ch. 3   *"Because of this omnivorousness as well as their intelligence, they have been able to survive the loss of forested land by adapting to human-made environments..."* North American Birds, National Audubon Society, 1984, p. 58.

Ch. 4   Lyrics from *Lola*, recorded by the Kinks, 1970, written by Raymond Douglas Davies © Hill and Range Songs, Inc. – BMI

Ch. 4   *"Monogamous. Solitary nester. Male feeds during courtship."* Birds of New England, Fred J. Alsop III, Smithsonian Handbooks, 2002, p. 226.

Ch. 5   *"Usually in pairs or flocks; especially gregarious after nesting season."* Birds of New England, Fred J. Alsop III, Smithsonian Handbooks, 2002, p. 226.

Ch. 6   *"They mimic the hawk's cry for no better reason, perhaps, than that they may laugh at the panic into which timid little birds are thrown at the terrifying sound."* Birds Every Child Should Know, Univ. of Iowa Press, Neltje Blanchan, 2000, p. 157 (orig. pub. 1907).

Ch. 7   *Chitty Chitty Bang Bang*, Song and movie based on Ian Flemming's book by the same name, © 1968 Metro-Goldwyn-Mayer Studios, Inc.

Ch. 7   *"Also musical 'weedle weedle', like the squeaking of a farm pump that needs oil. Variety of other vocalizations, some musical."* Birds of New England, Fred J. Alsop III, Smithsonian Handbooks, 2002, p. 226.

Ch. 8   *"Jays eat almost anything but prefer vegetable food, especially tree seeds, which are often buried for later consumption."* North American Birdfeeder Handbook, Robert Burton, National Audubon Society, 1995, p. 92.

Ch. 9   *"It eats many insects and is one of the few avian predators on hairy caterpillars."* Song and Garden Birds of North America, Alexander Wetmore, National Geographic Book Service, 1964, p. 138.

Ch. 10 *"Presented with new problems, [birds] appear to find the answers by a quick reorganization of their previous experience, without trials."* World of Birds, Fisher and Peterson, 1964, p. 159.

Ch. 11   *"Birds are creatures of instinct. ...and often are, improved by experience, by learning; and the learning and memory abilities of birds can be marvelous."* World of Birds, Fisher and Peterson, 1964, p. 157.

Ch. 12   *"It plucked an acorn, grasped it between its strong feet, and hammered the shell open with its sturdy beak."* Ranger Rick Magazine, National Wildlife Federation, Sallie Luther, April 1991, p. 23.

Ch. 13   Lyrics from *Old Cape Cod*, recorded by Patti Page, May 1957, Mercury Records #71101.

Ch. 13   *"Originally a bird of the wild woods, the blue jay has adapted itself to settlements of man."* Song and Garden Birds of North America, Alexander Wetmore, National Geographic Book Service, 1964, p. 138.

Ch. 14   *"It is often hard to ignore a bird that is wounded, exhausted, or orphaned, but most such birds are beyond saving."* North American Birdfeeder Handbook, Robert Burton, National Audubon Society, 1995, p. 205.

Ch. 15   *"They have a violent dislike of predators, and their raucous screaming makes it easy to locate a hawk or a roosting owl."* Field Guide to North American Birds, National Audubon Society, 1977, p. 553.

Ch. 16   *"The lives of most common birds are surprisingly short...In general it is the healthiest birds that survive the hazards of the first months of life and that continue the species."*   North American Birdfeeder Handbook, Robert Burton, National Audubon Society, 1995, p. 206.

Epilogue *"The hazards in a bird's life mean that it will be lucky to live beyond a couple of years."*   North American Birdfeeder Handbook, Robert Burton, National Audubon Society, 1995, p. 205.

Wildlife Resources

Coming upon an injured or orphaned bird can be a wrenching experience. Should you try to help? Should you leave the bird alone? If you do try to help, absolutely the most important thing is to get the bird to trained professionals as soon as possible. *Never try to help without expert advice.* Check the local telephone directory for rehabilitation centers and veterinarians. Call for information on where to bring the bird and what to do in the meantime. For general information, the Internet is a very valuable resource. Listed below are some of the many websites that provide information on caring for injured animals.

Association of Avian Veterinarians, www.aav.org

American Birding Assoc., www.americanbirding.org

U.S. Fish and Wildlife Service, http://birds.fws.gov

Audubon Society, www.audubon.org

Sierra Club, www.sierraclub.org

Int'l Bird Rescue Research Center, www.ibrcc.org

Rocky Mountain Raptor Program, www.rmrp.org

The Raptor Trust, www.raptortrust.org

Maryland Ornithological Society, www.mdbirds.org

Project Wildlife, www.projectwildlife.org/index.html

The Hummingbird Society, www.hummingbird.org

Raptor Education Group, www.raptoreducationgroup.org

Southeastern Arizona Bird Observatory,
www.sabo.org/index.htm

Miami Museum of Science, www.miamisci.org

Carolina Raptor Center, www.carolinaraptorcenter.org

Save Our Seabirds, www.seabirdrehab.org

TriState Bird Rescue & Research, www.tristatebird.org

Florida Fish & Wildlife Conservation Commission, http://floridaconservation.org

Audubon of Florida, www.audubonflorida.org/main/who.htm

National Aviary, www.aviary.org

Bird Observer, http://massbird.org/birdobserver

Audubon Society of Rhode Island, www.asri.org/index.html

Louisiana SPCA, www.la-spca.org/home.htm

Mountainaire Avian Rescue Society, www.wingtips.org

Wisconsin Humane Society, www.wihumane.com/index.html

California Acad. of Sciences, www.calacademy.org

Wildlife Rescue League, www.wildliferescueleague.org

Golden Gate Raptor Observatory, www.ggro.org

Angel Wings Waterfowl Rescue, www.waterfowlrescue.org/index.html

Oxley Nature Center, www.oxleynaturecenter.org/index.htm

Carolina Raptor Center, www.birdsofprey.org/home-page.htm

Bird Rescue of Oregon, www.rescuebird.com

Wildlife Rehabilitation Center of the North Coast, www.coastwildlife.org/index.html

The Feather, www.thefeather.org/index.htm

HolisticBird.org, www.holisticbird.org

Genesis Wildlife Sanctuary, www.genesiswildlife.org

WildlifeCare.org, www.wildlifecare.org

Suncoast Seabird Sanctuary, www.seabirdsanctuary.org/index.htm

New Jersey Audubon Society, www.njaudubon.org

257